Simple
Scrapbooks

digital designs
for scrapbooking

BY RENEE PEARSON

3

it takes a village

I used to think writing a book was a solitary affair. I'm here to tell you this book wouldn't have been possible without the help and support of a cadre of special people.

Kent, you're my husband, my lover and my best friend. Because you supported me, encouraged me, and even fed me, my dream has come true. You're my heart and soul and the very best part of me. I love you.

To the Primedia team.

Stacy Julian and Lin Sorenson, you two championed me and my digital ideas from the very start. Thank you for opening your arms and the pages of *Simple Scrapbooks* to me.

I'm thrilled to be a member of the team

Lynda Angelastro, you're a gem of an editor. I couldn't have asked for a better person to shepherd my book through the process from idea to reality. Kelley Lindberg, because of you the exercises in this book are coherent and easy to follow. Thank you both for your dedication.

Cathy Zielske and Don Lambson, you two rock! Your designs for this book give it the professional polish I always envisioned. I never worried for minute. Oh! And thanks for putting up with an art director's nightmare—an author who also happens to be a designer.

Chris, Tamara and Matthew, you're still the lights of my life. Sebastian, you're the reason I scrapbook. And to the rest of my family and friends, thank you for understanding my need to go "underground" until this book was finished. I'm back and I love you all. Let's party!

Renee

contents

a new set of tools

Have you ever felt not-so-confident about some aspect of your life and then met someone who clears the fog, gives you the insight and instruction you need and completely changes your outlook regarding that formerly confusing and discouraging aspect? I have. For some reason I've had all kinds of mental blocks against digital scrapbooking and yet I want to learn and I want to be competent. I want to use digital tools and techniques to help preserve my memories—I just needed some personal coaxing and a personal coach. Enter Renee Pearson. Renee is an expert—because one of her greatest joys is sharing her expertise, Renee is also a teacher. When she shared with me her concept for this book and showed me layer by layer how you could use Simple Schemes to create digital pages and albums, I felt a sudden surge of possibility and knew that I too could scrapbook beautifully and simply using my computer.

The skills that Renee taught me, and that she shares in this book, are just a new set of tools in my scrapbooking tool kit. I understand now that paper and digital scrapbooking each can enhance my ability to tell and share my story—and I can use both. And, that's exactly what I'm going to do.

Thanks Renee!

digital scrapbooking

Digital scrapbooking is one of the fastest-growing segments in the industry today. Go to nearly any scrapbooking website, and you'll find a digital section complete with chat rooms, galleries and downloads. Paper scrapbookers who, two or three years ago, discovered their computers were wonderful journaling tools, are now using applications like the Adobe Photoshop family to create digital page layouts every bit as stunning as those they design in paper.

As a professional graphic designer, I used to take the ability to use page layout and design applications for granted. But it didn't take many visits to online scrapbooking sites to notice how many scrapbookers wanted to learn to create pages digitally or add digital skills to their scrapbooking toolbox. While the popularity of digital scrapbooking has grown, learning materials have been hard to find. Books that teach digital software aren't written to teach digital scrapbooking or design.

digital designs for scrapbooking

I wrote *Digital Designs for Scrapbooking* to fill this gap. I wanted to make this book an all-in-one resource for would-be digital scrapbookers, with illustrated, step-by-step instructions for a variety of professionally designed scrapbooking projects. Because it's an ideal tool for digital scrapbooking, we'll be using Adobe Photoshop Elements. The templates, schemes and elements you need to complete your projects are on the CD that accompanies this book. I've even included a 30-day trial version of Adobe Photoshop Elements 3.0. And, when you're ready to design pages on your own, the CD contains digital Simple Schemes—easy-to-use page patterns—and four designer kits that contain well over 400 elements, all designed to make digital scrapbooking easier for you.

THE DESIGN COLLECTIONS

The four collections are named for places across the country that evoke a certain spirit and have influenced my own design style. Use these descriptions to help you choose which kit is right for your next project.

The Greenwich Collection I lived in Greenwich, Connecticut for several years and the Greenwich Collection has that same traditional New England flavor. It's ideal for holiday, heritage and wedding albums.

The Morningside Collection Morningside is home, it's the area of Atlanta where I now live and I love it. The Morningside Collection is eclectic, versatile and diverse, just like my neighborhood. It works well for lifestyle, relationship and casual albums.

The Oak Park Collection Oak Park, on Chicago's western border, is home to the largest collection of Frank Lloyd Wright-designed homes and buildings. The Oak Park Collection, like the place, has an urban traditional, hearth and home feeling about it. Use it for clean, simple lifestyle albums.

The Sedona Collection The Arizona desert is home to beautiful and awe-inspiring Sedona. The Sedona Collection reflects the town's spiritual, earthy, sensual and soulful presence. This collection is good for pages about self-discovery, life, exploration and travel.

I'm sure you'll find your own inspirations for these collections. I can't wait to see what you come up with.

using digital designs for scrapbooking

The first four chapters in this book are each designed to help you complete a different digital album and learn new digital design techniques. By completing these projects in order, you'll be creating your own digital scrapbook pages and learning a lot about Adobe Photoshop Elements in the process. While the screenshots were taken in a Windows environment, the instructions and elements work just as well if you're using a Mac. I chose Adobe Photoshop Elements for the projects in this book because, along with its big sister, Adobe Photoshop, it's the most popular digital scrapbooking tool. It's affordable and extremely

powerful. However, *Digital Designs for Scrapbooking* is not a technical Photoshop Elements how-to or a photo-editing manual. You'll find a few technical book recommendations at the end of Chapter Five.

In Chapter Five, you'll also find a wealth of time- and money-saving tips and tricks for preserving, printing and displaying your finished albums. *Digital Designs for Scrapbooking* also contains a gallery section where you can find completed projects from some of your favorite designers. Cathy Zielske, Donna Downey and Molly Newman have all used one of the collections to bring you an example of what they were able to do using my designs. And, at the end of the book is a catalog of the CD contents to help you find the item you want without having to comb endlessly through file folders.

so, digital or paper?

The good news is that today you don't have to choose one or the other. *Digital Designs for Scrapbooking* gives you everything you need to add digital scrapbooking to your toolbox. When you use those tools is up to you. In fact, you can even print out most of the CD images and use them for paper scrapbooking, or use them in other page layout or word processing programs! *Digital Designs for Scrapbooking* is about broadening your skills and horizons. It's that Simple.

photo-ready templates

Using photo-ready page templates is the easiest, fastest way to learn as you go. By the time you've finished this chapter, you'll have created a professional-looking scrapbook album. In addition, you'll have learned the basics of digital scrapbooking painlessly!

Photo-ready templates are complete scrapbook pages that are just waiting for you to drop in your own photos. Each page template is already laid out, color-coordinated, and embellished.

In this chapter, you'll create:

- A title page
- A dedication page
- A table of contents page
- A section page
- Filler pages

Collection: Morningside
Page Size: 6" x 6"

Unfamiliar with Photoshop Elements? Find demo and product highlight information on your Photoshop Elements CD, and extensive support under the applications' **Help** Button.

creating a title page

The first page of a scrapbook is usually the title page. An effective title page doesn't just name your scrapbook—it can also establish the theme, tone and color scheme you'll use throughout the scrapbook.

Follow these steps to create your own title page.

OBJECTIVES

- Locate and open photo-ready template files from the CD
- Enlarge the document window
- Save and rename files
- Locate your photo files
- Resize and position a photo on the page
- Use the **Type** tool to add a page title

STEP 1 Open Photoshop Elements and go to the Editor workspace.

If this is the first time you've used Photoshop Elements, a welcome screen appears. From the welcome screen select **Edit and Enhance Photos**. ❶ If the welcome screen doesn't appear, make sure you are in the Editor workspace. (If you're not, click the **Quick Fix** or **Edit Your Photo** icon, then click **Go to Standard Edit**.) Mac users: Your welcome screen will look slightly different. Click the **Close** button at the bottom of the window and continue on with the steps.

STEP 2 Find and open the title page photo-ready template *mstmplttl.jpg* on the CD.

Open the **File** menu and click **Open**. Go to the mstemplates folder of the Morningside Collection and double-click the *mstmplttl.jpg* file to open it. ❷

STEP 3 Enlarge the template to fit the screen.

From the **View** menu, click **Fit On Screen**. If nothing happens, your screen is already sized to fit the screen.

❶ **INFO TIP**

The template appears on a white background. Crop marks show on the white background at the template corners —these are for accurately trimming edge-to-edge layouts. For information about using crop marks, see Chapter 5.

STEP 4 Save the template and give it a new name so that it will become your title page.

From the **File** menu, click **Save As**. In the **Save As** dialog box, select the folder in which you want to create your scrapbook. In the **File Name** box, type *mytitle.psd*. In the **Format** box, select **Photoshop (*.PSD, *.PDD)**. Then click **Save**. ❸

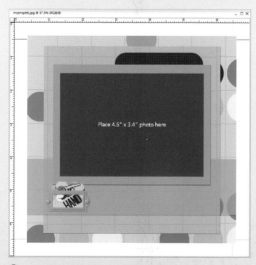

❶ *The Photoshop Elements welcome screen.*

❸ *The **Save As** window.*

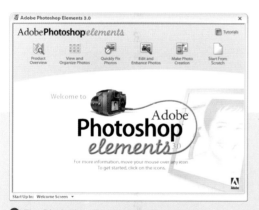

❷ *The title page photo-ready template.*

STEP 5 Find and open the photo file.

Go to the **File** menu, click **Open** and find a photo with a landscape (horizontal) orientation you to want use. You now have two files open in your workspace.

STEP 6 Copy and paste the photo onto your title page.

There are two ways to do this. You can drag and drop it, or you can copy and paste it. To drag and drop the photo onto the template, first click the **Move** tool icon ➤⊕ from the toolbox. (The toolbox is the set of icons to the left of the photo and template you're working with.) Then click the photo and drag it to the template.

To copy and paste the photo, from the **Select** menu click **All**. (Or you can click the **Rectangular Marquee** tool ⬚ from the toolbox and select the entire photo.) Then from the **Edit** menu, click **Copy**. Click the template, then from the **Edit** menu, click **Paste**.

The photo now appears on top of the template.

STEP 7 Close the photo file.

Now you should see just the template file with the photo pasted onto it. ❹

The right-hand side of the Editor is called the **Palette Bin**. When you first use the Editor, three palettes are visible by default: the **How To** palette, the **Styles and Effects** palette, and the **Layers** palette. Palettes let you manipulate your photos and projects in many ways. For now, we'll be using the **Layers** palette. To learn how to move these palettes around on the screen, minimize them, or replace them with other palettes, see the Adobe Photoshop Elements **Help.**

In the **Layers** palette, notice that the photo you pasted is shown as **Layer 1**. The template is the **Background layer**. Each photo or element you use on a page is a separate layer. You can work with each layer separately. You can make a layer transparent, so you can see through it to the layers beneath, or you can make a layer opaque, so you can't see

❺ *The photo layer is selected in the Layers palette.*

ⓘ **TECH TIP**

If you can't see the **Layers** palette fully, you can scroll through the layers, move the **Layers** palette to another part of your screen, or expand the **Layers** palette.

❹ *A photo has been pasted onto the template background.*

through it. We'll learn more about layers later. For now, we're going to work with the photo (**Layer 1**). ❺

STEP 8 Resize the photo to fit into the template.

From the toolbox, click the **Move** tool. The options bar across the top of the desktop changes to show the options you can use with the **Move** tool. Make sure **Auto Select Layer** is checked, then click the photo to select it. (The photo may already be selected.)

Position the photo so that its top left corner is aligned with the top left corner of the gray photo space in the template. ❻ From the **Image** menu, point to **Resize**, then click **Scale**. While holding down **SHIFT**, click the photo's bottom right corner handle and move the handle until the photo fits the gray space. (Holding down **SHIFT** keeps the photo from distorting as you resize.) If the bottom of your photo is off the page, move it up and align from bottom corner. ❼

ⓘ **TECH TIP**

It's best to only resize a large photo down to fit into a smaller space. Increasing the size of a small photo to fit into a larger space will decrease the resolution of the picture photo, lowering its quality.

STEP 9 Type a title onto your page.

From the toolbox, click the **Horizontal Type** tool [T]. The options bar across the top changes to show the options you can use with the **Type** tool. In the font box, select a font. (In my example, I used **Arial Black**.) In the size box, select a point size. (I used **60 point.**) Click the down arrow next to the **Color** box and select a color. (I used **darker warm brown**, at the bottom of the color swatches.)

Make sure the **Anti-aliased button**, right next to the type size box, is turned on (it will be shown in a white box if it is on). Anti-aliasing smooths out the edges of diagonal or curved lines by blending the edge pixels

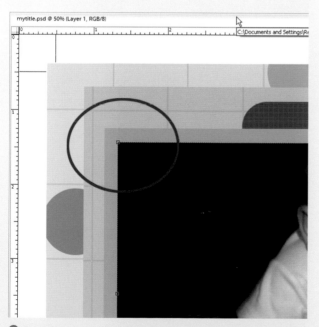

❻ *The left corner of the photo is in position.*

❼ *The photo has been resized and moved into place.*

between the item's color and the background color. ❽

Click in the area of the page where you want your title to begin. Type the title.

To move your title, click the **Move** tool, then drag the title to the location you prefer.

Notice that the text you typed has been added as a new layer to the **Layers** palette. ❾

STEP 10 Save your file.

From the **File** menu, click **Save**.

ℹ️ **TECH TIP**

When you save the file you'll see the message, "Turning off Maximize Compatibility may interfere with the use of PSD files in other applications or in future versions of Photoshop Elements." Make sure the Maximize Compatibility button is checked, then click OK. This ensures your file will be compatible with Photoshop CS as well as future versions of Photoshop Elements. If you wish, you can turn off this dialog through **Preferences** (under the **Edit** menu).

STEP 11 Close your file.

From the **File** menu, click **Close**.

Congratulations! You've just created your first page. Now you're ready for Lesson 2: Creating a Dedication Page.

❽ *Options are selected in the* **Type** *tool options bar.*

❾ *Completed title page.*

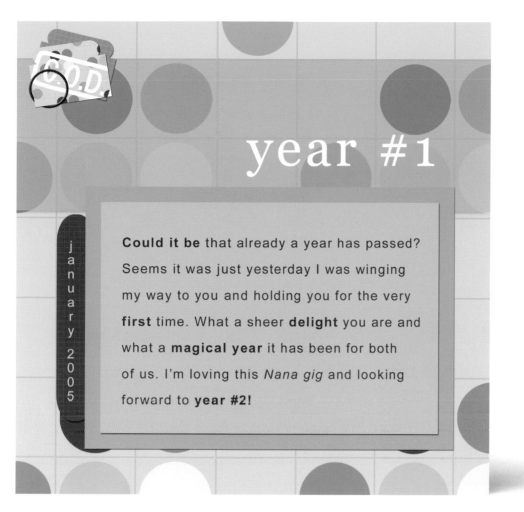

year #1

Could it be that already a year has passed? Seems it was just yesterday I was winging my way to you and holding you for the very **first** time. What a sheer **delight** you are and what a **magical year** it has been for both of us. I'm loving this *Nana gig* and looking forward to **year #2!**

january 2005

creating a dedication page

Your dedication page tells why you created this scrapbook—who it's for, or why this subject is important to you. You might include a quote or poem that sets the right tone, or just a bit of journaling to tell your story in your own words.

Follow these steps to create a dedication page.

OBJECTIVES

- Use the **Horizontal Type** tool to create a block of text
- Set alignment
- Set line-spacing (Leading)
- Use font attributes (bold, italics, etc.)
- Use **Faux Bold** & **Faux Italics**
- Use the **Vertical Type** tool
- Sample colors using the **Color Picker**

STEP 1 Find and open the photo-ready dedication page template *mstmplded.jpg* on the CD, in the mstemplates folder of the Morningside Collection.

STEP 2 From the **View** menu, click **Fit On Screen**.

STEP 3 Save the template with the new name *mydedication.psd*. Remember to save it in the **Photoshop (*.PSD, *.PDD)** format.

STEP 4 Use the **Horizontal Type** tool to type a title on the page. (See Step 9 in Lesson 1 for help typing and positioning your title.) ❶

STEP 5 Use the **Horizontal Type** tool to type your dedication text in the journaling area of the page. Before typing, remember to use the options bar to:

- Select your font, font size and color. (My example dedication page uses **Arial Regular**, **12 point**, in **darker warm brown**.)

- Ensure anti-aliasing is turned on.

- Click the **Left Align Text** button. This ensures the text will line up along the left margin, while the right margin of the text is staggered or "ragged." This allows for a consistent, natural spacing between words. Use hard returns to keep the right-hand side of the text inside the journaling area. If you turn on **Center Text**, each line of the text block will be centered. Centering is fine for titles or very short blocks of text, but not ideal for journaling blocks. **Right Align Text** will make the text line up at the right margin, but the left margin will be ragged. Choose this as an occasional design option, but usually not with journaling blocks.

- Change the leading setting if you prefer. Leading refers to the amount of space between lines, often called "line spacing." Click the **Leading** box and type or select the point size of space you want between lines. (My example uses **24 point** leading.) ❷

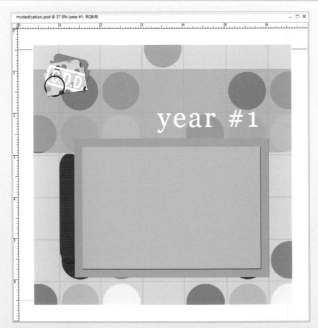

❶ *A title is added to the dedication page.*

How do you decide on a leading value? Here's a good rule of thumb: The smaller the type, the more leading you'll need. This is because tight (small) leading yields chunks of type that are difficult to read. Text needs "breathing room" on a page for our eyes to read it easily. For font sizes ranging from 8-12 points, make leading double the font size. For this exercise, I used **12 point** type with **24 point** leading.

STEP 6 Add a little visual interest by changing certain words to bold or italic type.

To change a word, be sure you're using the **Horizontal Type** tool and highlight the word like you would with a word processor. If the font you're using has its own bold and italic versions in its font family, click the **Font Style** box and select **Bold**, **Italic**, or **Bold Italic**. (Select **Regular** to change it back to regular font.) ❸

If your font family does not come with its own style versions, you can change the font style using

Photoshop Elements' **Faux Bold** or **Faux Italics** buttons. Faux (fake) styles are generated by your computer, and they approximate the font. If you have a choice, it's usually better to use the true font variants that come with your font family, but the faux versions are good alternatives. ❹ ❺

STEP 7 Use the **Move** tool to center the text in the journaling area.

Once you've clicked the **Move** tool, you can click anywhere in the box of text to move that text around on the page, just as you moved the photo.

STEP 8 Use the **Vertical Type** tool to add a vertical title to the tab just to the left of your journaling box.

Click and hold down the **Horizontal Type** tool. A menu of alternate type tools appears. ❻ The **Type** icon in

❸ *The Font style menu.*

mydedication.psd @ 24.2% (Lorem ipsum dolor sit amet, co, RGB/8)

❹ *In the Type tool options bar, Faux Bold is selected.*

Use a single space at the end of sentences. Double-spacing creates unattractive "rivers" of blank space in your text body. Double-spacing was needed with typewriters because their characters were mono-spaced (all letters take the same amount of space on the page). Most computer fonts, however, use proportional spacing based on the size and shape of the letters, so we no longer need to add two spaces after a period.

Could it be that already a year has passed? Seems it was just yesterday I was winging my way to you and holding you for the very **first** time. What a sheer **delight** you are and what a **magical year** it has been for both of us. I'm loving this *Nana gig* and looking forward to **year #2!**

❺ *Important words are bolded in the journaling text area.*

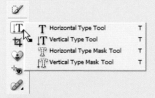

❻ *The Type tool with expanded hidden tools.*

the toolbox now has a vertical arrow next to it, indicating you've selected the **Vertical Type** tool. ┃T Position your cursor at the top of the tab and select your font and font size. ❼ Then type your tab title. Use the **Move** tool to position the title on the tab. ❽

STEP 9 Use the **Color Picker** to change the text color to the **cream** color of the page's background.

In the **Layers** palette, double-click the image of the text icon (called the layer thumbnail). The text on the tab is now highlighted.

In the **Type** tool options bar, click the **Color** box. The **Color Picker** appears, and the tool changes to an **Eyedropper.** ✎ Click the **Eyedropper** anywhere on the **cream** background of your page to select it, then click **OK.** ❾ The text is now **cream**. (You may have to click the **Move** tool to deselect the text and make the change take effect.) ❿

STEP 10 Save and close your file.

Now you've finished your dedication page, and you're ready to tackle your table of contents page.

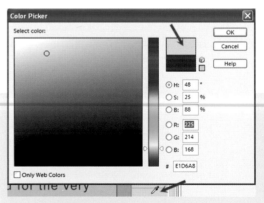

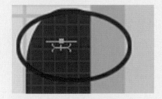

❼ *The cursor is in position to begin typing text onto the tab.*

❽ *The text is centered on the tab.*

❾ *The Color Picker is open and the Eyedropper is positioned over the cream-colored area.*

❿ *Completed dedication page.*

creating a table of contents

Occasionally, you'll add pages to your scrapbook that consist only of text, such as a table of contents page. One way to add visual interest to this kind of page is to change the opacity of a photo to make a soft background for the text.

Follow these steps to create a table of contents page.

OBJECTIVES

- Crop a photo to fit a space
- Turn layer visibility on and off
- Change the opacity of a layer to create a background

STEP 1 Find and open the photo-ready table of contents page template *mstmpltoc.jpg* on the CD, in the mstemplates folder of the Morningside Collection.

STEP 2 From the **View** menu, click **Fit On Screen**.

STEP 3 Save the template in Photoshop format with the new name *mytoc.psd*.

STEP 4 Find and open the photo you want to use in the background.

STEP 5 Copy the photo and paste it onto your title page. Then close the photo file.

STEP 6 Resize the photo, if necessary, so that the portion of the photo you want to use is about the same size as the table of contents space on the template background. (See Lesson 1, Step 8 for help resizing photos.) If your photo is still larger than the space,

continue steps 7-13 to learn to trim the excess.

STEP 7 In the **Layers** palette, click the **Eye** icon next to the photo layer. This turns off the photo layer's visibility so you can see the template behind it. ❶

STEP 8 From the toolbox, click the **Rectangular Marquee** tool  . Use the tool to carefully select the part of the table of contents area above the embellishment. (You may need to first use the **Zoom** tool 🔍 to zoom in on the table of contents area so you can see it better.)

STEP 9 Click the **Eye** icon next to the photo layer to make the photo visible again.

STEP 10 Move the bounding box until it's over the area of the photo you want to save. (If you zoomed in on the table of contents area before, zoom out to see the full page now. To zoom out hold down **Alt** and click.) ❷

❶ In the *Layers* palette, the *Eye* icon is turned off, making the photo invisible.

❷ A portion of the photo is selected with the *Rectangular Marquee* tool.

❸ The cropped photo is moved into place.

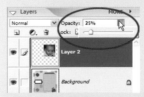

❹ The *Opacity* slider.

STEP 11 Remove the area of the photo that is outside the bounding box.

From the **Select** menu, click **Inverse**. Then from the **Edit** menu, click **Cut**.

STEP 12 Use the **Move** tool to move the photo to the table of contents box. ❸

STEP 13 Use the **Layers** palette to change the photo's opacity.

In the **Layers** palette, the **Opacity** box lets you set the opacity of a layer (in this case, our photo layer). Click the **Opacity** arrow, then move the slider to change the photo's opacity. In my example, I set the opacity to **25%**. ❹ ❺

STEP 14 Add a title, journaling, and a table of contents using the text techniques from previous lessons. ❻

STEP 15 Save your file. Notice that the **Layers** palette shows all the layers you've added to this page. ❼

STEP 16 Close the file.

You've finished your table of contents. Now it's time to make the rest of the pages of your scrapbook.

❺ The photo is set to **25%** opacity.

❻ The final table of contents page.

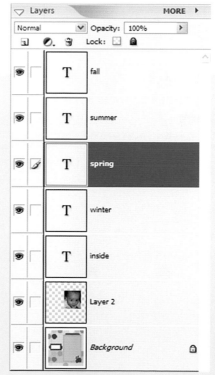

❼ The final **Layers** palette.

visiting morfar kurt - spring 2004

creating section and filler pages

You're now ready to complete the remaining pages of your album. One photo-ready template allows you to create a section page that introduces a section of your scrapbook. Two other templates let you create two different styles of filler pages. You can rotate or flip them to create additional page layouts instantly.

Follow these steps to create section pages.

OBJECTIVES

- Rotate templates to add variety to album pages
- Brief review of previous concepts & techniques

STEP 1 Open the section page photo-ready template *mstmplsec.jpg* on the CD, in the mstemplates folder of the Morningside Collection, and fit it to the screen.

STEP 2 Save the template in Photoshop format with the new name *mysection1.psd*. ❶

STEP 3 Using the techniques from previous lessons, add photos and a title to your section page.

STEP 4 Save and close your section page. ❷

Follow these steps to create a filler page. Repeat for as many filler pages as you need.

STEP 5 Find and open one of the two filler page photo-ready templates *mstmplfil1.jpg* or *mstmplfil2.jpg* on the CD in the mstemplates folder of the Morningside Collection, and fit it to the screen. ❸ ❹

Step 6 Save the template in Photoshop format with the new name *myfiller1.psd*.

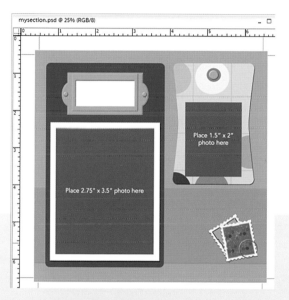

❶ *The section page photo-ready template.*

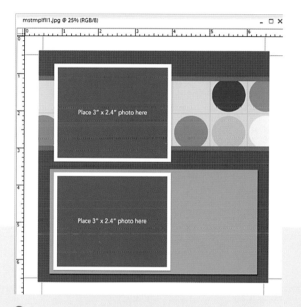

❸ *Filler page #1 photo-ready template (mstmplfil1.jpg).*

❷ *A completed section page.*

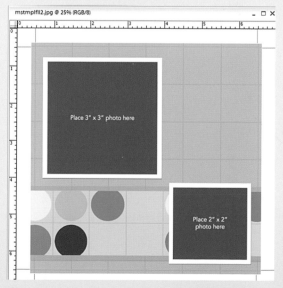

❹ *Filler page #2 photo-ready template (mstmplfil2.jpg).*

STEP 7 Rotate or flip the template to choose a page orientation.

From the **Image** menu point to **Rotate**, then click **90° Left**. This rotates the entire template a quarter-turn to the left. Also try selecting **90° Right**, **180°**, **Flip Horizontal** and **Flip Vertical**, or combinations of rotating and flipping to see the different looks you can create.

Think about how the page will look side-by-side with another page, and plan the orientation so that a two-page spread appears coordinated. ❹ ❺ ❻ ❼

STEP 8 Save and close your filler page.

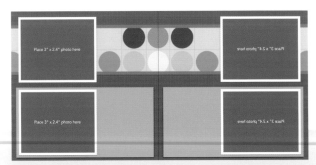

❹ *Filler template #1. The left page is original orientation; the right page is flipped horizontally.*

❻ *Filler template #2. The left page is rotated **90 degrees right**; the right page is rotated **90 degrees left**.*

❺ *Filler template #1. The left page is rotated **90 degrees left**; the right page is rotated **90 degrees right**.*

❼ *Filler template #2. The left page is rotated **90° left**; the right page is rotated **90° left** then flipped horizontally.*

in the hammock

a beautiful spring day and
what could be more fun
than experiencing the joys
of a hammock with tant
cecilia.

REVIEW

Congratulations! In this chapter, you've created your own digital scrapbook! And along the way, you've learned how to:

- Open, rename, and save files
- Add, resize, and position photos on a page
- Add text to a page
- Crop photos
- Change the opacity of a layer
- Rotate pages

In the next chapter you'll learn how to create your own pages with Simple Schemes layouts using all the techniques you've already practiced.

everything's an adventure.
even mamma's and pappa's
bed can be a playground
filled with delights. seeing
this photo let us know
you weren't a tiny baby
any longer. you were
becoming an explorer.

on the bed

ready, set, done!

title page

sebbe

dedication page

year #1

january 2005

Could it be that already a year has passed? Seems it was just yesterday I was winging my way to you and holding you for the very first time. What a sheer delight you are and what a magical year it has been for both of us. I'm loving this Nana gig and looking forward to year #2!

table of contents

inside

winter

spring

summer

fall

section page

spring

visiting morfar kurt - spring 2004

filler page

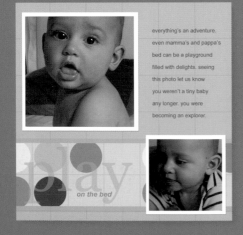

everything's an adventure. even mamma's and pappa's bed can be a playground filled with delights. seeing this photo let us know you weren't a tiny baby any longer. you were becoming an explorer.

play

on the bed

filler page

fun

in the hammock

a beautiful spring day and what could be more fun than experiencing the joys of a hammock with tant cecilia.

using simple digital schemes

In Chapter 1, you created albums using photo-ready page templates. Now you're ready to build layered pages using Simple Schemes.

Simple Schemes appear in each *Simple Scrapbooks* magazine. They're blueprints designed to make building page layouts quick and easy. The schemes in this project make a coordinated scrapbook album. Everything you need is here: title, dedication, table of contents, section layouts and two filler pages. As in Chapter 1, you can rotate the filler pages for variety.

In this project you'll learn how to turn Simple Schemes into 8.5 x 11 digital scrapbook pages. We'll use the Oak Park Collection which is perfect for the clean, graphic scrapbooking style that's so popular.

In this chapter, you'll create:

- A title page
- A dedication page
- A table of contents page
- A section page
- Filler pages

Collection: Oak Park
Page Size: 8.5" x 11"

You'll replace each of the layers in the Photoshop Elements files with items from the digital collection to create these stylish pages.

Most home printers can't print an image that covers the paper's entire surface because of the rollers that advance the paper through the printer. While edge-to-edge printed pages are nice, you can accommodate this printer limitation by purposely adding a white border. That's exactly what I've done with this Simple Scheme set. (If your printer does print edge-to-edge, the CD contains an identical set of background pages without the white border that you can use instead.)

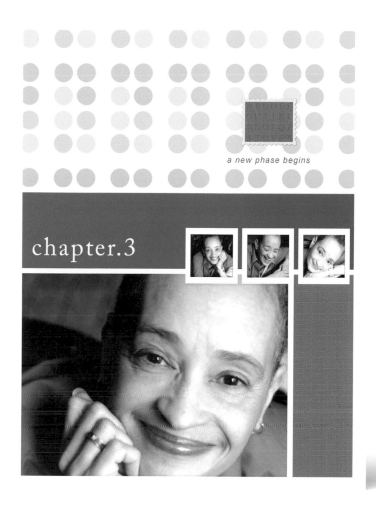

a new phase begins

chapter.3

LESSON ONE

creating a title page

Follow these steps to create your own title page.

(See Chapter 1 for help with any of the Photoshop

Element tools and techniques we covered there.)

OBJECTIVES

- Stack layers to build page layouts
- Copy items from one document window to another
- Delete layers
- Fill portions of a layer with sampled color
- Lock transparent areas of layers
- Add decorative elements

STEP 1 Find and open the title page scheme *85schmttl.psd* on the CD, in the Schemes folder, 85x11schemes subfolder, and rename it *schemetitle.psd*. This renamed file will be your scrapbook page. ❶

Look at the **Layers** palette. ❷ Each item on the page has its own layer. Think of them as layers of paper and embellishments on a traditional scrapbook page. The bottom layer (named "white background" in this Simple Scheme) is the equivalent of the background paper for your page.

Some layers, like the background layer, cover the entire page. Others appear to cover only a portion of the page, but actually they have some filled pixels (the ones you see) and some transparent pixels (the ones you don't see).

Imagine you have a stack of 8.5 x 11 pieces of glass. Each piece of glass has something painted on it. When you stack them, you can see the entire composition through the clear areas. Each layer in Photoshop

Elements is like one piece of glass, and the clear areas are the transparent pixels. The bottom layer is the bottom piece of glass. To make something on one piece of glass appear on top of another piece of glass, you move it up in the stack. This will all make sense as we build the scrapbook page .

Because our design incorporates a white border, we don't need to replace the white background layer. The first element we'll replace is the pattern area at the top of the page.

STEP 2 Select the pattern area to be replaced.

The easiest way to do this is to use the **Layers** palette. In the **Layers** palette, select the pattern layer. Then hold down **CTRL** (**CMD** on a Mac) and click the pattern layer's icon (called the layer thumbnail, located just

❶ *The title page Simple Scheme.*

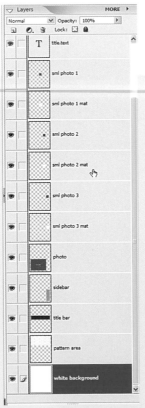

❷ *The **Layers** palette.*

above the white background layer). A selection marquee now surrounds the area on the page that you'll be replacing.

STEP 3 Open the *opbgrnd1c.jpg* background file from the opbackgrounds folder in the Oak Park Collection on the CD. This file is the patterned "paper" you'll use to replace the pattern layer in the scrapbook page. Arrange the two document windows so you can see both of them.

STEP 4 Drag the selection marquee from your scrapbook page to the patterned background paper.

To do this, click your scrapbook page so that you can work with it (notice that the pattern area is still highlighted by the selection marquee) and choose the **Rectangular Marquee** tool. Drag the selection marquee from the scrapbook page onto the background file's window.

Position the marquee where you want it over the pattern. Remember, whatever you see inside the marquee is what you'll be copying onto your scrapbook page. ❸

STEP 5 Copy the selected portion of the patterned paper, then paste it onto your scrapbook page.

A new layer, called **Layer 1**, has been added to the **Layers** palette above the pattern area layer.

STEP 6 You can delete the old pattern area layer by dragging it up to the **Trash** button at the top of the **Layers** palette. (Or you can select the pattern area layer and click the **Trash** button, then click **Yes** when asked if you want to delete the layer.) ❹ Then close the pattern background file.

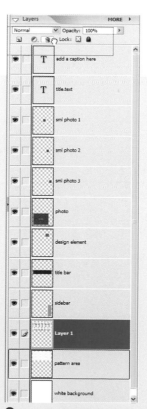

❸ The rectangular marquee is positioned over the background pattern.

❹ To delete the old pattern area layer, drag it to the *Trash* button.

STEP 7 Use the same techniques to replace the sidebar with different patterned "paper" from the file *opbgrnd2c.jpg.*

First, select the sidebar layer in the **Layers** palette. Then create a marquee around the sidebar by pressing **CTRL** (**CMD** on a Mac) and clicking the layer's thumbnail. Open the *opbgrnd2c.jpg file.* Choose the **Rectangular Marquee** tool and drag the marquee from your scrapbook page to the background paper. Then copy the background paper and paste it onto your scrapbook page. Finally, delete the old sidebar layer from the **Layers** palette. Then close the backgound file. ❺

STEP 8 Change the color of the title bar to match the **blue** in the dots of the patterned background.

To ensure the entire title bar layer isn't filled with color, first lock the layer's transparent pixels (the ones you can't see, remember?). To do this, select the title

bar layer in the **Layers** palette. At the top of the **Layers** palette, you'll see the word "**Lock**" and two buttons: a padlock (which says "**Lock all**" when you position the mouse over it) and a small square (which says "**Lock transparent pixels**" when you position the mouse over it). Click the square button (the **Lock transparent pixels** button). This locks the transparent pixels so they stay transparent. (If you click the **Padlock** icon, the entire layer will be locked and you won't be able to change the layer at all.) ❻

Now you can change the color of the title bar. From the **Edit** menu, click **Fill Layer.** When the **Fill Layer** dialog box appears, click the arrow next to the **Use** list, and choose **Color.** The **Color Picker** will appear. ❼ Move the mouse to your scrapbook page, and notice that the cursor changes to an **Eyedropper.** Position the

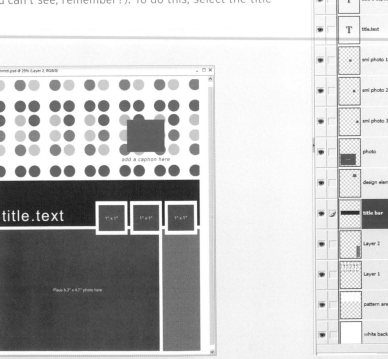

❺ The original sidebar has been replaced with the new background paper

❻ Click the **Lock transparent pixels** button in the **Layers** palette to ensure the transparent pixels in a layer stay transparent

Eyedropper over one of the **blue** dots on your scrapbook page and click. Click **OK** to close the **Color Picker,** then click **OK** again to close the **Fill Layer** dialog box. Now the title bar should appear **blue**.

STEP 9 Open the *opstamps.png file* from the CD, in the opelements folder in the Oak Park Collection.

This file contains decorative elements (faux postage stamps) that you can add to your scrapbook page. You'll replace the **blue** square in the top half of your scrapbook page (the design element layer) with one of the stamps from this file.

STEP 10 Copy and paste a stamp onto your scrapbook page.

To easily position the stamp on the page, first select the **blue** decorative element square by holding **CTRL**

(**CMD** on a Mac) and clicking the decorative element layer thumbnail in the **Layers** palette. Then, in the stamp file, use the **Rectangular Marquee** tool to draw a marqee around the second stamp from the left in the top row. ❽ Copy the selection and use **Paste Into Selection** to paste it onto your scrapbook page. It will appear on top of the **blue** square.

STEP 11 Remove the **blue** square from your page by deleting the decorative element layer from the **Layers** palette. Then close the stamp file. ❾

STEP 12 Using the techniques from Chapter 1, select each photo layer and add a corresponding photo to your scrapbook page. Crop or resize the photos as required. When you finish adding the photos, delete their corresponding placeholder layers.

There is a separate placeholder layer for each photo on this page. When you add a photo to the page, remember it will become a new layer. To make sure

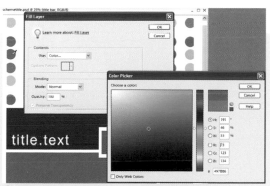

❼ The *Fill Layer* and *Color Picker* dialog boxes.

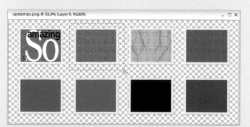

❽ The opstamps.png *file contains faux postage stamps you can use to decorate your scrapbook page.*

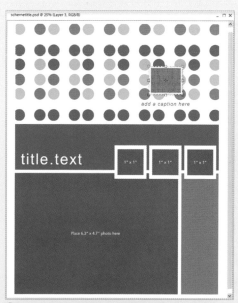

❾ *A faux postage stamp has been added to the scrapbook page.*

you can see the new photo, you always want to create the new photo's layer ABOVE the placeholder layer.

To do this, select the placeholder layer in the **Layers** palette BEFORE you paste the photo onto the page. If you don't select the placeholder layer first, the photo you paste may appear hidden behind the placeholder layer. If this happens, don't worry. You can use the **Layers** palette to move the photo layer so that it's on top of the placeholder layer: simply drag the photo layer up in the palette until it's above the placeholder layer.

STEP 13 Using the techniques you learned in the first chapter, add a title and a caption.

STEP 14 Look at your scrapbook page and make any additional changes, such as reducing a layer's opacity.

As you look at your scrapbook page, you may decide you want to go back and modify something you've already done. For example, now that our page is complete, the background circles in the top half of the page seem to be competing with the photos for attention. Since we want the photos to be the focal point of our page, let's go back and reduce the opacity of the pattern layer.

In the **Layers** palette, select the pattern layer, **Layer 1**. Then click the **Opacity** arrow in the **Layers** palette and move the slider to change the paper's opacity to **30%**.

STEP 15 Save your file.

You've finished your title page! ❿ You started with a Simple Scheme, and modified the colors and decorative elements to create your own page. Now you're ready to create a dedication page.

❿ *The completed title page.*

ⓘ **TECH TIP**

When using the **Rectangular Marquee** tool, you can select a perfect square by holding down the **SHIFT** key as you drag the marquee across your photo.

ⓘ **DESIGN TIP**

My Oak Park Collection scheme uses the **Arial** font for the title and caption, but you can replace it with any font you like. I replaced the title font in my page with **Adobe Caslon Pro**.

It's funny when I think about it. I'm finally getting to know me...really getting to know me. Who knew that turning fifty would open a whole new world to me? I feel as though I'm finally hitting my stride with nothing to prove to anyone but myself. It's a wonderful time...it's a beautiful feeling.

hello.me

when i smile,
life smiles back

june 2005

LESSON TWO

creating a dedication page

Now, you'll create your dedication page by replacing the scheme's layers with items from the CD and with your own photos. You'll start with the bottom layer and move up. We'll also begin manipulating your photos to create new effects.

The following steps will help you to create your personal dedication page.

OBJECTIVES

- Convert color photos to black and white
- Adjust the brightness and contrast of a photo
- Merge layers
- Fill a layer with color

STEP 1 Find and open the dedication page scheme *85schmded.psd* on the CD, in the Schemes folder, 85x11schemes subfolder, and rename it *schemeded.psd*. We'll call this renamed file your scrapbook page. ❶

STEP 2 Select the pattern layer by holding down **CTRL** (**CMD** on a Mac) and clicking the pattern layer thumbnail in the **Layers** palette.

STEP 3 Open the background file *opbgrnd1c.jpg* from the opbackgrounds folder of the Oak Park Collection.

STEP 4 Replace the pattern area with the dots background paper.

Use the **Rectangular Marquee** tool to drag the selection marquee from your scrapbook page to the patterned background paper. Then copy the selected portion of the pattern and paste it onto your scrapbook page. Use the **Layers** palette to reduce the background layer's opacity to **30%**. Delete the old

pattern layer and close the background file.

STEP 5 Use the same steps to replace the two sidebar areas with the background from the file *opbgrnd2c.jpg*. (Leave the opacity at **100%**.) ❷

STEP 6 Open a color photo and convert it to black and white.

Find and open the photo you want to use for the bottom photo layer. From the **Image** menu, point to **Mode**, then click **Grayscale**. When asked if you want to discard color information, click **OK**. Your photo now appears in black and white. ❸

STEP 7 Because digital photos converted to grayscale often are lacking in contrast and appear washed out, correct this by adding a brightness/contrast adjustment layer to your image.

Still working in your photo window, click the **Create**

❶ The dedication page Simple Scheme.

❷ The pattern and sidebar layers have been replaced.

ℹ **TECH TIP**
Adjustment layers let you experiment with color and make tonal adjustments without permanently modifying an image. Learn more about them in Adobe Photoshop Elements **Help**.

adjustment layer button at the top of the **Layers** palette and choose **Brightness/Contrast**. Now, play around with the sliders until you're satisfied with your photo, then click **OK**. ❹ ❺

STEP 8 Copy and paste your adjusted photo onto your scrapbook page. Crop and resize the photo as necessary.

Because you added an adjustment layer to your photo, you can't just drag and drop your photo into the layout as usual—if you do, you'll only capture one of the layers. To capture both layers of the corrected photo, use the **Copy Merged** command.

First, select the portion of the photo you want to copy. From the **Select** menu click **All** to copy the entire photo. To copy a portion of the photo that matches the size of the placeholder, hold down **CTRL** (**CMD** on a Mac) and click the placeholder photo layer in your

scrapbook page. Then use the **Rectangular Marquee** tool to drag the marquee onto your photo. Position the marquee over the portion of the photo you want to copy.

After you've selected the photo, go to the **Edit** menu and click **Copy Merged.**

Next, make sure the photo placeholder layer in your scrapbook page is selected, then paste the merged photo as usual (from the **Edit** menu, click **Paste Into Selection**).

STEP 9 Delete the placeholder photo layer from the **Layers** palette.

STEP 10 Repeat the same steps to replace the middle photo layer with your own black and white photo, then delete the placeholder photo layer.

STEP 11 Copy, paste and resize a color photo and place it over the small photo layer in your scrapbook page.

❸ From the *Image* menu, point to *Mode*, then click *Grayscale* to convert a color photo to black and white.

❹ The *Create adjustment layer* button in the *Layers* palette lets you modify a photo's brightness and contrast

ⓘ DESIGN TIP

The photos I wanted to use for this album were all shot in color, so I converted them to black and white. Using black and white adds a bit of sophistication to the page. Plus I don't have to worry about colors in my photos clashing with the colors of my layout, and I can bring continuity to photos taken at different times under different lighting conditions.

❺ Adjust the sliders in the *Brightness/Contrast* dialog box.

Then delete the placeholder photo layer. 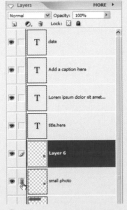 ❻

STEP 12 Link the photo layer with the small photo mat placeholder layer below it.

Because file sizes can get large in Photoshop Elements, it's often a good idea to reduce the number of layers. One way to do this is to merge layers. In this case, we can merge the small photo layer with its white mat. Remember, after two layers are merged, you can no longer separate them and work with them individually.

In the **Layers** palette, select the new photo layer. Then look at the mat layer. The column immediately to the left of the mat layer's icon has a small blank square in it. Click the square, and a **Link** icon will appear. The mat layer is now linked to the selected photo layer. ❼

STEP 13 To merge the layers, open either the **Layer** menu or the **Layers palette** menu, then click **Merge**

Linked. (To display the **Layers palette** menu, click **More** at the top of the **Layers** palette.) ❽

STEP 14 Instead of using a photo to replace the last photo placeholder at the top of the page, let's change its color and make it a color bar.

To make the photo placeholder a color bar, you simply change its color. You don't need to replace the placeholder layer with another layer. We're going to use one of the colors in the circular pattern background, but first we need to raise the background's opacity back to **100%**.

First, select the background's layer in the **Layers** palette and use the opacity slider to increase the layer's opacity back to **100%**. Next, select the **Eyedropper** tool from the toolbox, then click one of the **turquoise** circles in the background. Notice that the foreground color in the toolbox changes to **turquoise**. Now lower the background layer's opacity

❻ *Three photos are added to the scrapbook page.*

❼ *The link icon indicates that the layers are linked in the Layers palette.*

ⓘ **DESIGN TIP**

To add contrast to my page I left one photo, the smallest one, in color. This adds a bit of visual interest to the page.

ⓘ **TECH TIP**

When layers are linked, you can move their contents together. You can also copy, paste, merge, and apply transformations to all linked layers simultaneously. To learn more about linking, refer to Adobe Photoshop Elements **Help.**

back to **30%**.

Before filling the color in the photo layer, we need to lock the transparent pixels of that layer so that they don't get filled with color, too. In the **Layers** palette, select the top photo layer and click the **Lock transparent pixels** button. ⑩

Now, from the **Edit** menu, point to **Fill Layer,** and the **Fill Layer** dialog box appears. In the **Use** list, select **Foreground Color.** Leave the **Mode** setting as **Normal,**

and leave the **Opacity** at **100%.** Then click **OK.** The photo space is now filled with **turquoise** color. ⑪

STEP 15 Using the techniques from Chapter 1, add a title, journaling, a caption, and a date. ⑫

STEP 16 Save your file.

You're done with your dedication page now! Next, you'll build a table of contents page for your album.

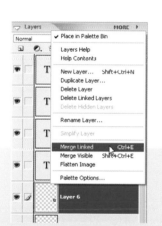

⑧ The Layers palette menu

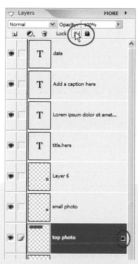

⑩ When you click the **Lock transparent pixels** button, a lock icon appears in the layer

 ⑨ The Eyedropper tool is positioned over a turquoise circle, and the foreground color in the toolbox has changed to match.

ⓘ DESIGN TIP

Simple Schemes give you a worry-free way to change the elements on the page to suit your own ideas and creativity. Although the Simple Scheme for this page calls for a fourth photo, we can change our mind and use that space for something else instead, without fear that the page will look unbalanced.

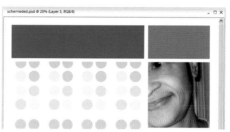

⑪ The photo space in the top photo layer is now filled with color instead of a photo.

⑫ The completed dedication page.

.woman
.mother
.artist
.dreamer

creating a table of contents page

Previously, you learned that you can resize a photo using the **Move** tool. You can also use the **Rectangular Marquee** tool to crop a photo to size. But Photoshop Elements includes a third way to resize a photo—specify the exact measurements or a percentage and the program will resize the photo for you.

Replace the scheme's layers with items from the CD and with your own photos. It's usually easiest to start with the bottom layers and move up the **Layers** palette. Follow these steps to create your table of contents page.

OBJECTIVES

- Use the **Resize** command to change the size of photos
- Recolor the photo mat in a placeholder layer

STEP 1 Open the table of contents page scheme *85schmtoc.psd* from the Schemes folder, 85x11schemes subfolder, on the CD and rename it *schemetoc.psd*. ❶

STEP 2 Use the same background file, *opbgrnd1c.jpg*, to replace the pattern layer. Remember to reduce the background layer's opacity to **30%**.

STEP 3 Fill the top bar layer with the **turquoise** color, just as you did in Step 14 in Lesson 2. ❷

STEP 4 Select the middle photo layer. Open and copy a photo onto this layer.

STEP 5 Select the photo layer. Then from the **Image** menu, point to **Resize**, then click **Scale**.

Handles appear on the edges and corners of the photo. You can use these handles to resize the photo manually, but we're not going to do that this time. Notice that the option bar above the document window changes to show the options available with the **Scale** command.

In the options bar you'll see that the image is **100%** of its width and **100%** of its height.

STEP 6 In the options bar, change the width and height scales from percentages to inches by right-clicking (holding **CTRL** and clicking on a Mac) both boxes and choosing **inches**. ❸

STEP 7 Click the link icon between the width and height boxes. This is the **Maintain aspect ratio** button, and it will keep the photo proportional as you change one dimension or the other.

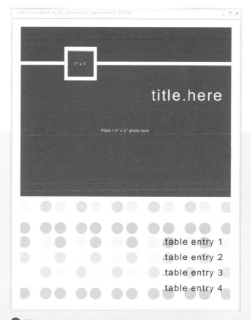

❷ *The background and top bar are completed.*

❸ *In the Resize options bar, right-click (hold CTRL and click on a Mac) the width and height boxes to change the display from percentages to inches.*

❶ *The table of contents simple scheme*

STEP 8 To match the gray photo space, enter either **7.9 inches** for the width, or **5 inches** for the height, depending on which dimension is more appropriate for the photo you're using.

As you enter one dimension, note that the other dimension changes automatically, because you chose to maintain the aspect ratio. You probably will need to crop one dimension of the photo to make it fit the space. ❹

STEP 9 Use the **Move** tool to position the photo.

STEP 10 Crop the photo to fit, if necessary.

To trim away the excess, first click the **Eye** icon next to the photo layer in the **Layers** palette to turn off the photo layer's visibility. Use the **Rectangular Marquee** tool to select the gray photo area. Click the **Eye** icon next to the photo layer to make the photo visible again. From the **Select** menu, click **Inverse**.

Then from the **Edit** menu, click **Cut**.

STEP 11 When you finish positioning the photo, delete the placeholder layer.

STEP 12 Select the small photo layer, then add a small photo to the page. Size or recrop the photo using whichever methods you prefer.

In our next step, we will change the color of the mat for this small photo.

STEP 13 Use the **Eyedropper** tool to choose a color for the small photo's mat.

Select the background layer and increase its opacity to **100%**. Use the **Eyedropper** tool to click on one of the **salmon**-colored circles. Now the foreground color

❹ *If you click the **Link** icon to maintain the photo's aspect ratio, you can enter a new value for the width, and the height value will change automatically.*

ℹ **TECH TIP**

An aspect ratio is an image's height-to-width relationship. When working with photos, always make sure you maintain the aspect ratio—unless you're deliberately going for a distorted look, which can sometimes be fun!

ℹ **TECH TIP**

You can also use the **Resize/Scale** command to resize a photo by percentages instead of inches. Sometimes when I'm resizing I'm not sure exactly how much I want to change it, so I use the percentage resizing instead of actual measurements. For example, if I have a very large object I need to fit into a smaller space, I can click the **Maintain aspect ratio** button and then enter **50%** in either the width or height box. If the resized image is too small, I raise the percentage by small increments. If it's still too big, I reduce it until it's what I'm looking for. I also do this when I have an object that's slightly larger than I need. I usually reduce it **1%** at a time until I get what I want.

is changed to **salmon**. Change the layer's opacity back to **30%**.

STEP 14 Create a marquee around the small photo's mat layer by holding down **CTRL** (**CMD** on a Mac) and clicking the placeholder layer's icon in the **Layers** palette.

STEP 15 From the **Edit** menu, click **Fill Selection**. Make sure the **Use** list shows **Foreground Color**, leave the **Mode** setting as **Normal**, and leave the **Opacity** at **100%**. Then click **OK**. The mat behind the photo now appears **salmon**. ❺

STEP 16 Using the techniques from Chapter 1, add a title and your table of contents information. ❻

STEP 17 Save your file.

Another page finished! Now you're ready to create your section and filler pages.

❻ *The completed table of contents page.*

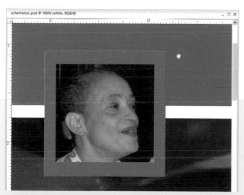

❺ *The mat area behind the small photo is now filled with color.*

ⓘ TECH TIP

You can either keep the placeholder layer and the photo layer as separate layers (in case you decide to change the color of the mat again later), or you can merge them. If you choose to merge them, see Step 12 in Lesson 2 for instructions.

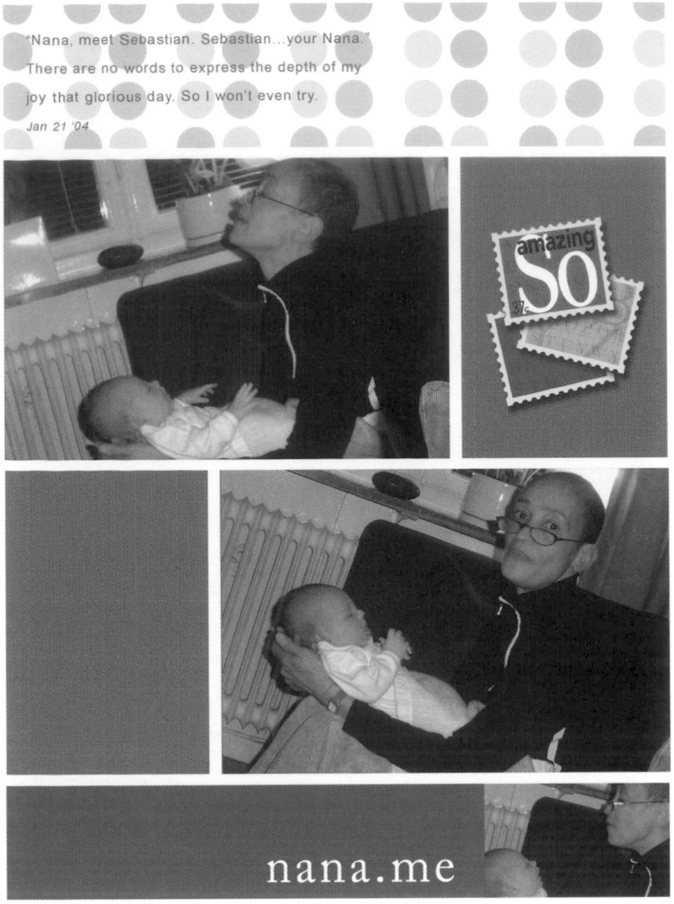

"Nana, meet Sebastian. Sebastian...your Nana."
There are no words to express the depth of my
joy that glorious day. So I won't even try.

Jan 21 '04

nana.me

creating section and filler pages

You've now learned how to turn a Simple Scheme into a personalized scrapbook page.

But what if you'd like to modify the scheme a little or add a few embellishments from the CD? In this lesson you'll learn how to selectively rotate and rearrange the elements in a Simple Scheme layout. Let's use one of the filler pages to demonstrate these techniques.

OBJECTIVES

- Change the orientation of page elements
- Use the **Styles and Effects** palette
- Combine elements
- Add drop shadows

ⓘ INFO TIP

This chapter's Simple Scheme contains two filler pages and a section page. We'll only use one of the filler pages for the instructions in this lesson, but feel free to explore your creativity using the other filler page and section page!

For this lesson, let's use Filler Page #2. I'd like to flip this layout vertically so the faded pattern is on the top instead of the bottom. Then I want to flip it horizontally so the journaling begins on the left instead of the right. It seems like I could do this very quickly by using the **Image** menu to flip the page vertically and then horizontally. The only problem is that my journaling text would end up reversed and upside-down. That's not what I want! I want to rearrange everything *except* my text layer. Here's how I'll do it:

STEP 1 Open the filler page scheme *85schmfil2.psd* from the Schemes folder, 85x11schemes subfolder, on the CD. ❶

STEP 2 Select the pattern layer, then link all of the layers above it except the text layer. Leave the text layer unlinked. (There's no need to change the white background layer.)

To link layers to the selected pattern layer, click the box in the column to the left of each layer's thumbnail in the **Layers** palette. All of the layers you clicked plus the pattern layer are now linked together. Any rearranging you do to one will affect the others. ❷

STEP 3 Flip the linked layers vertically.

In the **Layers** palette, select any one of your linked layers. From the **Image** menu, point to **Rotate**, then click **Flip Layer Vertical**. ❸

Now the pattern layer is at the top of my layout. By linking the other layers you've ensured that the relationship of the layers to the layout as a whole has been preserved.

STEP 4 (Optional) Flip the linked layers horizontally.

In the **Layers** palette, select any one of your linked layers. From the **Image** menu, point to **Rotate**, then click **Flip Layer Horizontal**.

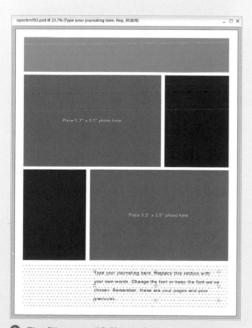

❶ The filler page #2 Simple Scheme.

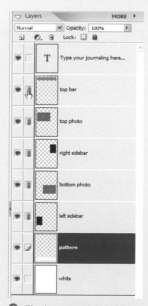

❷ The **Layers** palette shows the non-text layers linked to the pattern layer.

❸ From the **Image** menu, point to **Rotate**, then click **Flip Layer Vertical**.

STEP 5 Use the **Move** tool to position the text layer at the top left of the layout. ❹

STEP 6 Unlink the layers by selecting the pattern layer and clicking the **Link** icon beside each linked layer.

ⓘ **INFO TIP**

You can keep these layers linked if you like, but remember to unlink them if you want to work with the layers individually.

STEP 7 To save this version of the scheme for future use, from the **File** menu, click **Save As** and give it the name *myscheme.psd*.

STEP 8 Your scheme is now ready to use. Just as you did in the previous lessons, replace the scheme's layers with items from the CD and your own photos.

Use the same background file, *opbgrnd1c.jpg*, to replace the pattern layer (and remember to reduce its opacity to **30%**). Use the file *opbgrnd2c.jpg* to replace the sidebar layers. ❺

STEP 9 Let's add three of the postage stamp elements to the page. First, open the *opstamps.png* file from the *opelements* folder in the Oak Park Collection. ❻

STEP 10 Select one of the sidebar layers.

STEP 11 Select three stamps and copy each of them into your layout.

❹ *The rearranged scheme.*

❺ *Photos and patterns have been added to the rearranged filler page*

ⓘ **TECH TIP**

If you can't see your stamps because they paste in behind a photo, simply drag the stamp layer to a higher position in the **Layers** palette.

ⓘ **DESIGN TIP**

To balance my page, I filled the top bar layer (which is now on the bottom of the page) with **turquoise**, then pasted a small photo over one portion of the bar. You can add a photo if you like, or you can leave the bar as a solid color, depending on the look you want.

To copy a stamp, use the **Rectangular Marquee** tool. Draw a selection around your first stamp, then copy and paste it into your layout. Repeat for more stamps. When you are finished, close the stamp file. ❼

STEP 12 Arrange the stamps on your page.

Try a variety of techniques until you're satisfied with your arrangement:

- If the stamp you want on top is beneath the others, drag its layer to the top of the stack in the **Layers** palette.

- To rotate a stamp slightly, first select the stamp's layer. Then, from the **Image** menu, point to **Rotate,** then click **Free Rotate Layer.** A bounding box appears around the stamp. Move the pointer outside the bounding border until it becomes a curved, two-sided arrow. Drag the arrow until you're satisfied with the rotation.

- Use the **Move** tool to position the stamps where you want them. ❽

STEP 13 Add drop shadows to the stamps.

ⓘ **DESIGN TIP**

I've already added slight shadows to the stamps to give them depth, but you can add even more.

To add shadows to an element, use the **Styles and Effects** palette in the **Palette Bin.** First, select one of

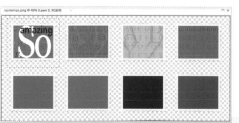

❻ The opstamps.png file contains images of faux stamps.

❽ The top bar layer with the stamps arranged.

❼ The page with stamps pasted over the sidebar layer.

the stamp layers in the **Layers** palette. Then expand the **Styles and Effects** palette. You'll see two drop-down lists at the top of the **Styles and Effects** palette. In the first drop-down list, select **Layer Styles**. In the second drop-down list, select **Drop Shadows**. ❾ Choose one of the drop shadow styles in the window. (I chose **Low** for the example page.) Repeat these steps to add drop shadows to the other two stamps. ❿

STEP 14 Add journaling and a title to the page. ⑫

STEP 15 Save your file.

STEP 16 Add additional filler pages and section pages using all the techniques you've learned so far.

❿ *The postage stamps now have drop shadows.*

❾ *Select the **Low** drop shadow style from the **Styles and Effects** palette*

ⓘ **TECH TIP**

You may have to expand the **Styles and Effects** palette to see all of your choices. To do this, click the triangles at the top left of the **Layers** palette and the **How To** palette to minimize those palettes. The **Styles and Effects** palette will then be expanded.

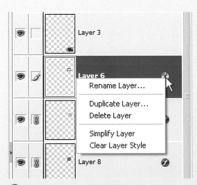

⓫ *Right-click (hold **CTRL** and click on the Mac) the stamp layer to remove layer styles*

ⓘ **TECH TIP**

To remove a drop shadow, right-click (hold **CTRL** and click on a Mac) the stamp layer in the **Layers** palette. From the menu that appears, choose **Clear Layer Style**. ⓫

"Nana, meet Sebastian. Sebastian...your Nana."
There are no words to express the depth of my
joy that glorious day. So I won't even try.

Jan 21 '04

nana.me

⑫ *The completed filler page.*

REVIEW

Can you believe what you've accomplished? In this chapter, you've used Simple Schemes to create and customize the pages of your own digital scrapbook. While putting together beautiful pages, you've learned how to:

- Move, replace and delete layers
- Lock transparent pixels in layers
- Fill portions of a layer with sampled color
- Convert color photos to black and white
- Adjust the brightness and contrast of a photo
- Merge layers
- Use **Resize** to size photos to exact dimensions
- Recolor the photo mat in a placeholder layer
- Add and modify decorative page elements
- Use the **Styles and Effects** palette
- Add drop shadows

In the next chapter you'll learn how to create your own Simple Schemes.

picture-perfect pages!

title page

a new phase begins

chapter.3

dedication page

It's funny when I think about it. I'm finally getting to know me . really getting to know me. Who knew that turning fifty would open a whole new world to me? I feel as though I'm finally hitting my stride with nothing to prove to anyone but myself. It's a wonderful time . it's a beautiful feeling.

hello.me

when i smile,
life smiles back

June 2005

table of contents

who.i am

.woman
.mother
.artist
.dreamer

section page

.dreamer

dreams,
if they're any good
are always a little
crazy.
ray charles

filler page

Nana, meet Sebastian. Sebastian , your Nana. There are no words to express the depth of my joy that glorious day. So I won't even try.
Jan 21 '04

So

nana.me

filler page

A dreamer then, a dreamer now. Who is this beautiful young woman? So full of hopes and plans. So young. So happy and confident. So young. So excited to face the future. So young. Life was an adventure then and it still is. A dreamer then, a dreamer now. So young...

sweet.sixteen

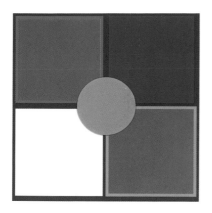

creating your own digital simple schemes

In Chapter 2, you used a set of Simple Schemes to create a beautiful scrapbook. The project in this chapter is also based on a Simple Scheme design. But instead of starting with pre-made page layouts, you'll start this project by creating your own digital Simple Scheme.

You've already learned most of what you need to know, and building your own schemes will give you a library of page ideas to draw from when planning your own digital layouts.

In this chapter, you'll create:

- A simple scheme
- A title page
- A dedication page
- A table of contents page
- A section page
- Filler pages

Collection: Sedona
Page Size: 8" x 8"

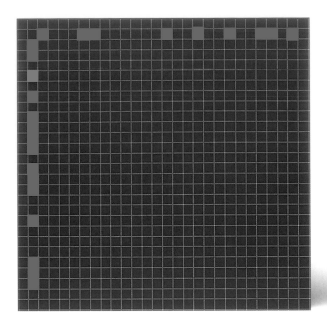

preparing to build a simple scheme

In this lesson you'll begin creating your own Simple Schemes and get a behind-the-scenes peek at my design process.

On the *Digital Designs for Scrapbooking* CD, there are four sets of Simple Schemes. Two of the Simple Scheme sets are for 8 x 8 pages, one makes 6 x 6 pages, and the remaining set makes 8.5 x 11 pages. For this lesson, you'll recreate the title page for one of the 8 x 8 Simple Schemes, so that you can see how I put it together.

OBJECTIVES

- Turn on rulers and grids
- Reset rulers zero origin point
- Load a color swatch palette
- Rename layers
- Add layers

In the Extras folder on the CD, you'll find basic page templates with crop marks for different sizes of pages. We'll use one of these files to begin creating our title page.
Let's get started!

STEP 1 Find and open the file *8x8template.png* from the Extras folder on the CD and save it as *my8x8scheme.psd*.

Make sure you save it as a Photoshop Elements (.psd) file. (It will default to .png because the file you opened was a .png file.)

STEP 2 To make it easier to keep your design balanced and your elements aligned, turn on rulers.

From the **View** menu, click **Rulers**. A ruler appears along the top and left sides of the document window.

STEP 3 Again, to help keep your elements aligned, turn on the grid and set it to ¼" increments.

From the **View** menu, click **Grid**.

From the **Edit** menu, point to **Preferences**, then click

Grid to display the **Preferences** dialog box. (On a Mac, from the **Photoshop Elements** menu, point to **Preferences**, then click **Grid**.) In the box beside **Gridline every**, enter **1**. Then from the drop-down list in the next box, click **inches**. In the box beside **Subdivisions**, enter **4**. ❶ This will set your document window to display a gridline every inch with four subdivisions, giving you a ¼" grid to work with. ❷

STEP 4 Although your finished page size will be **8 x 8** (after you crop it) the document size right now is actually **8½ x 8¾** because of the crop marks layer. Let's align your rulers with the boundaries of the finished page size instead of the boundaries of the document. First, use the **Zoom** tool to zoom in on the upper left corner of your image until you reach **100%** magnification.

You can either keep clicking the upper left-hand corner of the page until the **Zoom** box in the options bar

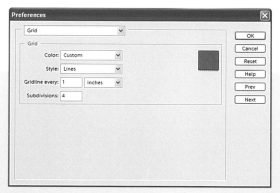

❶ Use the *Preferences* dialog box to set the grid dimensions.

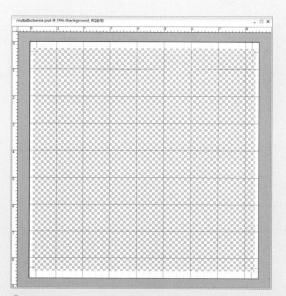

❷ The document window shows rulers and grid turned on.

shows **100%**, or you can type **100%** in the **Zoom** box, then reposition your page until you see the upper left-hand corner.

STEP 5 From the **View** menu, click **Grid** to turn off the grid so that you can move the rulers more freely.

STEP 6 The rulers' current origin point (0) is the upper left corner of the image. In the upper left corner of your image window, near the rulers, are crosshairs where the rulers intersect. Click and hold the mouse button and drag these crosshairs until they are aligned with the crop marks, then release them. The new zero origin point is set. ❸

If you miss it the first time, ignore the lines you just drew, click the crosshairs up in the left corner of the window again, and try again until you're satisfied.

STEP 7 Turn the grid back on and zoom out again so you can see your entire image.

STEP 8 The only layer in our page so far is named **Layer 0**. Change this layer's name to *crop marks* by double-clicking **Layer 0's** name in the **Layers** palette. Type the new name and press **Enter**.

STEP 9 Click the **Create a new layer** button at the top of the **Layers** palette to create a new layer and rename it *background*. ❹ You can also create a new layer by clicking the **More** button to display the **Layers** palette menu, then clicking **New Layer**.

STEP 10 Drag the crop marks layer to the top of the **Layers** palette. Remember to always keep this layer at the top. ❺

STEP 11 From the **Windows** menu, click **Color Swatches** to open the **Color Swatches** palette. ❻ When you create a new scheme, you must choose colors to represent the different elements on the page, such as the background, mats, and title bar.

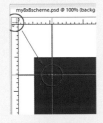

❸ *Change the rulers' zero origin point by dragging the crosshairs until they line up with the crop marks.*

❹ *The Create a new layer button.*

ⓘ TECH TIP

You can turn the grid off and on as often as you wish. Choosing **Grid** from the **View** menu toggles the grid on and off. You can also toggle the rulers on and off.

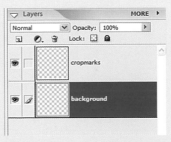

❺ *Drag the crop marks layer to the top of the Layers palette.*

The CD contains a palette of color swatches that I created and use for all of my schemes. To use my swatches for your elements, replace the default swatches in the **Color Swatches** palette with mine.

STEP 12 On the **Color Swatches** palette, click the **More** button, then click **Load Color Swatches**. ❼

STEP 13 In the **Load** dialog box, locate the *simple_ schemes.aco* file, then click **Load**. My color swatches are now displayed. ❽*

I've given you six colors plus **black** and **white**. Let's use **dark blue** to fill in the background layer.

STEP 14 Select the background layer in the **Layers** palette.

STEP 15 Click the **dark blue** swatch in the **Color Swatches** palette to make it the foreground color. (Hover the mouse over a color swatch to display the

color's name.) When you click a color in the **Color Swatches** palette, it appears as the foreground color in the toolbox. ❾

ⓘ TECH TIP

At the bottom of the toolbox, you'll notice two color boxes. The top box contains the foreground color and the bottom box contains the background color. These boxes are always "loaded" with either the default colors (black and white) or colors you've selected by clicking on a color swatch or by using the **Eyedropper** tool to sample colors within your image. If you click the double-arrow next to the color boxes, the foreground and background colors will reverse. If you click inside either box, the **Color Picker** will open, allowing you to choose another color.

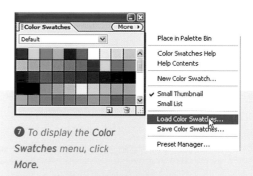

❼ *To display the Color Swatches menu, click More.*

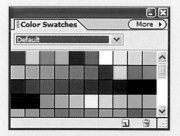

❻ *The default Color Swatches palette.*

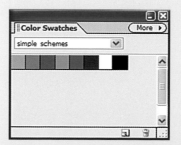

❽ *The Simple Schemes color swatches.*
*This .aco file is **not** on your CD, download it from www.simplescrapbooksmag/download/digital.*

❾ *The foreground and background color boxes in the toolbox.*

STEP 16 From the **Edit** menu, point to **Fill Layer**. Select **Foreground Color**. Leave the **Mode** setting as **Normal**, and leave the **Opacity** at **100%**. Then click **OK**. ❿

STEP 17 Save your file.

Continue designing and building your scheme in Lesson 2.

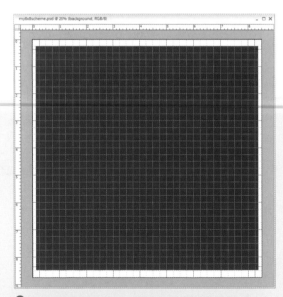

❿ *The background layer is filled with **dark blue**.*

designing and building your simple scheme

In this lesson you'll continue designing and building your own Simple Scheme from the file you created in Lesson 1. Review the last lesson, if necessary, to make sure your file is ready for the next step.

Now, follow these steps to watch your Simple Scheme take shape!

OBJECTIVES

- Use **Snap to Grid**
- Create photo mats using shape layers
- Simulate a vellum overlay
- Create drop shadows "from scratch"
- Use the **Gaussian Blur** filter

STEP 1 If it's not open already, find and open the file you created in the previous lesson (*my8x8scheme.psd*). ❶

STEP 2 Make sure the grid and rulers are turned on, that the zero origin point is still set to match the crop marks, and that the Simple Schemes color swatches are loaded. (See Lesson 1 for help.)

ⓘ **TECH TIP**

The zero point origin reverts to its original point outside the boundaries of our page every time you close the file, so you'll have to reset it each time you open the file.

STEP 3 From the **View** menu, click **Snap to Grid**. This ensures your cursor is pulled to the nearest grid mark when you are drawing or moving elements.

STEP 4 Now you're going to add a photo mat in the lower right-hand corner of your page. First, select the background layer in the **Layers** palette, so that the photo mat layer will be added above it. ❷

STEP 5 Click and hold the mouse button over the **Custom Shape** tool ⬚ in the toolbox. (If you've used one of the other shape tools before this lesson, its icon will appear in the toolbox instead of the **Custom Shape** tool, so click and hold that button instead.) From the menu of shape tools that appears, click **Rectangle tool**. ▭ ❸

STEP 6 Because you're going to make this photo mat **light blue**, click the **light blue** swatch in the **Color Swatches** palette.

Not only is the foreground color in the toolbox now **blue**, so is the **Color** box in the options bar. ❹ The **Color** box is also now loaded with the color swatches you're using. Click the arrow next to the **Color** box to display the swatches. This is where you'll select your foreground colors as you build additional layers.

❶ The Simple Scheme page you created in the previous lesson

❸ *When you click and hold the Shape tool button in the toolbox, a menu of shape tools appears*

❷ *The background layer is selected.*

ⓘ **TECH TIP**

Another way to select the **Rectangle** shape tool is to click the **Shape tool** in the toolbox, then click the **Rectangle** tool in the options bar that appears. Use whichever method you prefer to select the **Rectangle** shape tool.

STEP 7 Using the rulers and grid as guides, use the **Rectangle** shape tool to draw a square in the lower right-hand corner of the page.

Before you begin drawing the square, look at the rulers. Because this is an **8** x **8** page, the exact center of your page is **4"** on the horizontal ruler and **4"** on the vertical ruler. (Make sure you've adjusted the rulers' zero origin point to line up with the crop marks, or these dimensions will be off.)

Position your cursor in the exact center of the page, using the rulers as guides. Click and drag the mouse toward the bottom right corner of the page to draw a square from the center that measures **3⅞"** on each side. (Stop drawing when both the horizontal and vertical rulers indicate you've reached the **7⅞"** mark.) You may need to zoom in on the page to get the grid to let you work with ⅛" markings.

STEP 8 In the **Layers** palette, double-click on the name of the new layer you just created and rename it *lower right mat*. ❺

STEP 9 Now click the arrow beside the **Color** box in the options bar to display the color swatches, and click **medium blue**. Use this color for the top left mat.

STEP 10 You'll make this mat just slightly smaller than the first mat. To draw this mat, begin at the ⅛" marks in the top left corner of the page, and drag the square until it reaches **3⅞"** on both rulers. ❻

STEP 11 Rename this layer *top left mat*.

STEP 12 Now draw another rectangle to indicate a block of digital "vellum" in the upper right corner of the page.

Draw this rectangle using the same **medium blue** as the top left mat. Begin at the **4⅛"** mark on the horizontal ruler and the ⅛" mark on the vertical ruler. Stop drawing at the **7¾"** mark on the horizontal ruler and **3⅞"** on the vertical ruler. This will give us room to add a drop shadow.

STEP 13 To make this mat look like vellum, reduce its opacity to **30%**.

ⓘ INFO TIP

You can use shape tools to draw lines, rectangles, ellipses, other shapes and even custom shapes in Photoshop Elements. To learn more about shape tools, see Adobe Photoshop Elements **Help**.

❹ The *Color* box in the options bar turns *light blue* when you select *light blue* from the *Color Swatches* palette.

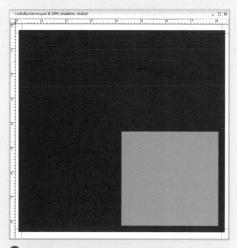

❺ The Simple Scheme layout with the first photo mat.

STEP 14 Rename this layer *vellum*.

STEP 15 The next step is to add a shadow behind the vellum. Click the **Create a new layer** button and rename the new layer *shadow*.

You could use Photoshop Elements' **Drop Shadow Layer Style** from the **Styles and Effects** palette, but I want to show you how to make your own shadows from scratch. This technique will give you more control over shadow.

STEP 16 Position the new shadow layer so it's just beneath the vellum layer. Make sure it's still selected.

STEP 17 Press and hold **CTRL** and click (**CMD** on a Mac) the vellum layer's thumbnail in the **Layers** palette.

The shadow layer should still be selected, since that's the layer you're still working with, even though you've just created a selection marquee around the vellum rectangle. That marquee will determine where the pixels will be filled on the shadow layer.

STEP 18 From the **Edit** menu, click **Fill Selection**. In the **Use** box, select **Black** and click **OK**. ❼

STEP 19 Select the **Rectangular Marquee** tool, then click inside the selection to deselect it.

STEP 20 Click the **Eye** icon beside the vellum layer in the **Layers** palette to turn off the vellum layer's visibility while we concentrate on the shadow.

STEP 21 Select the **Move** tool. Now, instead of using the mouse to move the shadow, use the arrow keys on your keyboard to move it. Press the **RIGHT ARROW** key on your keyboard three times to move the shadow layer three positions to the right, then press **DOWN ARROW** three times to move the shadow three positions down.

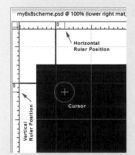

❻ *Begin drawing the second mat by positioning the cursor at the ⅛" marks on the rulers.*

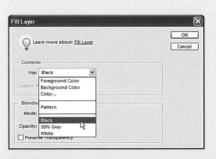

❼ *The Fill Layer dialog box.*

❶ DESIGN TIP

One of Adobe Photoshop Elements' neat features is its capacity to simulate "real world" elements, such as vellum. By using opacity and drop shadows, you can create pages with realism and depth.

STEP 22 To blur shadow, run the **Gaussian Blur** filter.

From the **Filter** menu, point to **Blur** then click **Gaussian Blur**. The dialog box that appears lets you control how far the blur extends. First, make sure the **Preview** box is checked so you can see your changes before you commit to them.

The **Preview** window is currently zoomed in on a small portion of the shadow layer. Use the mouse to drag inside the preview window until you can see a corner of your shadow. You can also click the + and – buttons to zoom in and out.

Adjust the slider and note how the blur extends as you slide back and forth. ❼ Stop when you reach **8.0** pixels. (You can also type **8.0** in the **Radius** box.) Then click **OK**.

STEP 23 Now, delete the portion of the shadow that's still underneath the vellum. With the shadow layer still selected, press and hold **CTRL** (**CMD** on a Mac) and click the veluum layer's thumbnail. Press delete to remove that portion of the shadow.

ⓘ TECH TIP

When you're creating drop shadows from scratch, you only need to delete the potion under your original layer if you're changing the opacity of that layer. Otherwise you can leave it.

Change the shadow layer's opacity to **20%**.

STEP 24 Click the **Eye** icon beside the vellum layer to turn the vellum layer's visibility back on .

STEP 25 Turn off the grid to see what your page looks like so far. ❽

STEP 26 Save your file.

In the next lesson, you'll finish adding elements to your layout.

❼ The *Gaussian Blur* filter dialog box.

ⓘ INFO TIP

The blur filters soften a selection or an image. **Guassian Blur**, one of the five blur filters, quickly blurs a selection by an adjustable amount. To learn more about the blur filters, see Adobe Photoshop Elements **Help**.

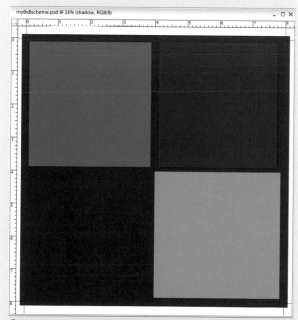

❽ *Your Simple Scheme layout so far*

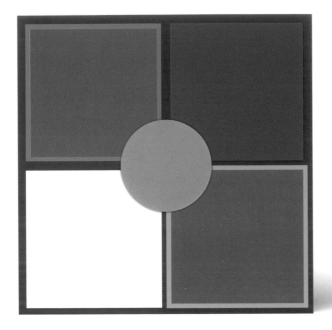

completing your simple scheme

In this lesson you'll finish building the title page scheme by adding design embellishments. Review the last lesson, if necessary, to make sure your file is ready for the next step.

Now, follow these steps to finish your Simple Scheme.

OBJECTIVES

- Use the **Elipse** tool to draw perfect circles
- Edit the effects of a layer's style
- Simplify shape layers

STEP 1 If it's not open already, find and open the file you built in the previous lesson (*my8x8scheme.psd*). ❶

STEP 2 Make sure the grid and rulers are turned on, that the zero origin point is still set to match the crop marks, and that the Simple Schemes color swatches are loaded. Remember to turn on **Snap to Grid**. (See Lessons 1 and 2 for help.)

STEP 3 Select the lower right mat layer in the **Layers** palette. We're going to add a photo layer on top of this mat layer.

STEP 4 In the **Layers** palette, click the **Create a new layer** button and rename the new layer *lower right photo*.

STEP 5 Load the foreground color with **dark gray** by clicking the **dark gray** swatch in the **Color Swatches** palette.

STEP 6 Load the background color with **white** by clicking once on the background color box in the toolbox, then clicking on the **white** swatch in the **Color Swatches** palette. ❷

STEP 7 Use the **Rectangle** shape tool to draw a rectangle for the bottom right photo.

Begin drawing at the **4⅛"** marks on both the horizontal ruler and the vertical ruler and end at the **7¾"** marks. If you can't see your new layer, make sure it's above your lower right mat in the **Layers** palette.

Remember, you may need to zoom in on the document to be able to work with ⅛" marks.

STEP 8 Add a new layer on top of the top left mat layer, and rename it *top left photo*.

STEP 9 Use the **Rectangle** shape tool to draw a rectangle for the top left photo.

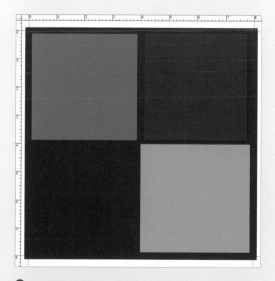

❶ The Simple Scheme page you created in the previous lesson.

❷ The foreground color box in the toolbox is loaded with *dark gray* and the background color box is loaded with *white*.

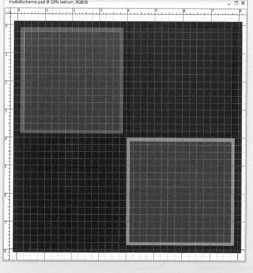

❸ Two photo layers have been added to the layout.

Begin drawing at the ¼" marks on both the horizontal ruler and the vertical ruler, and end at the **3¾"** marks. If you can't see your new layer, make sure it is above your top left mat in the **Layers** palette. ❸

STEP 10 Add a new layer, and rename it *journaling*. This journaling box will go in the bottom left corner of the page. There is no mat in that corner, so it doesn't matter where this layer sits in the stack as long as it's above the background layer.

STEP 11 Make sure the **Rectangle** shape tool is still selected.

STEP 12 Switch the foreground and background colors by clicking the double-headed arrows next to the **Color** boxes in the toolbox.

STEP 13 Use the **Rectangle** shape tool to draw a

rectangle for the journaling box.

Begin the rectangle at the ⅛" mark on the horizontal ruler and the **4⅛"** mark on the vertical ruler. End the rectangle at **3 ⅞"** on the horizontal ruler and **7⅞"** on the vertical ruler. ❹

STEP 14 Now you're going to add a layer for the circle element in the center of the page. This layer must be on top of all the mat, photo, and journaling layers, but just below the crop marks layer. Therefore, in the **Layers** palette, select the layer that is just below the crop marks layer.

STEP 15 Add a new layer and rename it *circle*. ❺

STEP 16 Select the **Ellipse** shape tool.

If you still have the **Rectangle** shape tool selected, click the **Ellipse** shape tool in the options bar. If not, click and hold the **Shape** tool in the toolbox and select the **Ellipse** tool from the menu that appears.

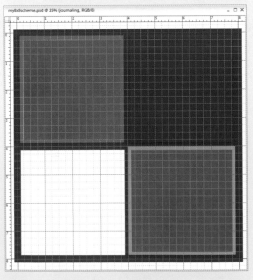

❹ *The **white** journaling block has been added to the page layout.*

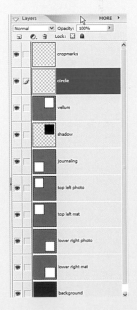

❺ *Make sure the circle layer is on top of all the photo, mat, and journaling layers, and just below the crop marks layer in the **Layers** palette.*

STEP 17 In the options bar, click the down-arrow by the shape tools. This displays a dialog box of **geometry options** for the shape tool you have selected. ❻

STEP 18 Click **Circle** (which lets you draw a perfect circle) and **From Center** (which lets you draw a circle outward from its center).

STEP 19 In the **Color** box in the options bar, select **light gray**.

STEP 20 Position the cursor in the exact center of your page, at the **4″** marks on both rulers.

Click and drag your cursor to the **5¼″** mark on the horizontal ruler. You don't have to worry about the vertical ruler because you selected the option to draw a perfect circle. ❼

Next you'll add a shadow to the circle.

STEP 21 Turn off the grid. (From **View**, click **Grid**.)

STEP 22 Select the circle layer in the **Layers** palette.

STEP 23 From the **Styles and Effects** palette, click the **Low** drop shadow style. If necessary, zoom in on your circle so you can see its shadow well.

STEP 24 Now you can modify the shadow style by changing the shadow's lighting angle and the distance it extends from behind the circle. In the circle layer in the **Layers** palette, double-click the small "**f**" icon.

This displays the **Style Settings** dialog box, which lets you control the shadow. ❽ First, make sure the **Preview** box is checked so you can see your changes before you commit to them.

STEP 25 Click the arm on the **Lighting Angle** dial and drag it to move it around the dial while looking at the

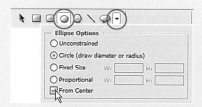

❻ The *Ellipse tool* and the **geometry options** down-arrow on the options bar.

ⓘ TECH TIP

Sometimes, when you create a new layer on top of another layer, the new layer will pick up attributes of the layer below it. For example, when you draw a circle layer above the vellum layer, your circle may suddenly appear with the same reduced opacity as the vellum layer. If this happens, simply raise the circle's opacity back to **100%**.

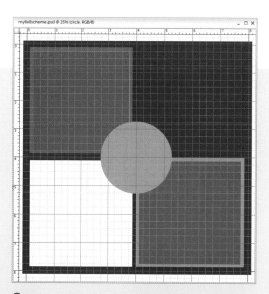

❼ The circle layer is added to the page.

shadow of the circle on your page. Notice the shadow moves based on where the dial is pointing. Set the angle to **120°**. (You can drag the dial until it shows **120°**, or you can type **120** into the box by the dial.)

STEP 26 If it's not already selected, click the box next to **Use Global Light**.

STEP 27 Change the shadow's distance by moving the slider until you're satisfied. The example uses a distance of **8 pixels**. Then click **OK**.

ⓘ **INFO TIP**

In Photoshop Elements, you can simplify shape layers, type layers and other types of layers. Simplifying a layer turns it into an image layer. One benefit of turning shape layers into image layers is that it reduces the size of the file. Another benefit is that you can only apply filters to image layers. We'll learn more about filters in the next chapter.

STEP 28 Now you can "simplify" your photo, mat, and journaling layers, because you won't be changing those layers anymore. (Do not simplify the circle layer or the vellum layer, however, because you'll be modifying those layers in a later lesson.)

To simplify the journaling layer, select the layer in the **Layers** palette. Then, from the **Layers** menu, click **Simplify Layer**. Repeat for the lower right mat, lower right photo, top left mat and top left photo layers.

STEP 29 Save your file. ❾

In the next lesson, you'll learn more about Photoshop Elements techniques as you build a page based on your new scheme.

❽ The *Style Settings* dialog box lets you set the shadow's angle and distance.

ⓘ **INFO TIP**

The **Lighting Angle** setting simply simulates the effect of a light source shining on your image from the direction, or angle, you choose. For example, a **120°** angle simulates a light source shining from the upper left. The **Use Global Light** option applies the lighting angle to all styles in the image. To learn more about Style Settings, refer to Adobe Photoshop Elements **Help**.

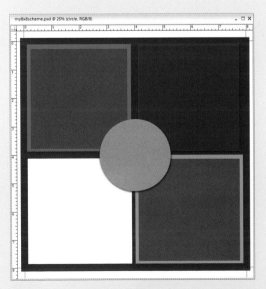

❾ The completed Simple Scheme.

creating a page using your simple scheme

Now that your own digital Simple Scheme is finished, it's time to use the elements from the Sedona Collection to create a page with it. Review the last lesson, if necessary, to make sure your file is ready.

Now, follow these steps to create your page.

OBJECTIVES

- Change layer content colors quickly
- Use transparent overlays from the CD collection
- Add to selections
- Use **Undo** and **Redo** operations

STEP 1 If it's not open already, find and open the file you built in the previous lesson *my8x8scheme.psd*, and rename it *sedonatitle.psd*. ❶

STEP 2 If you like working with the grid and rulers, make sure they are turned on and that the zero origin point is set to match the crop marks. Remember to turn on **Snap to Grid**. (See Lessons 1 and 2 for help.)

STEP 3 Load my Sedona color swatches from the Extras folder on the CD.

If necessary, open the **Color Swatches** palette by clicking **Color Swatches** in the **Window** menu. Then click the **More** button on the **Color Swatch** palette, then click **Load Color Swatches**. Find and load the *sedona.aco* swatches from the Extras folder on the *Digital Designs for Scrapbooking* CD. ❷

ⓘ DESIGN TIP

In addition to the color swatches you used to make your Simple Scheme page in the previous lessons, I've also provided color swatch sets for each of the design collections. These sets will make matching your own backgrounds and mats to the collections easy.

STEP 4 Using the skills you've already learned, add photos to your page. You may want to rename your layers as you add them. It helps to keep you from getting confused. Remember to delete the photo placeholder layers as you replace them with your photos. ❸

ⓘ DESIGN TIP

I like to add my photos first, since they're the foundation for my page and will determine my background and color choices.

❷ The Sedona *Color Swatches* palette.

❶ The Simple Scheme page you created in the previous lesson.

❸ Photos have been added to the page.

STEP 5 Change the color of the background layer to **dark teal** from the Sedona swatches palette.

Select the background layer. In the **Color Swatches** palette, click **dark teal** to make it the foreground color. Then from the **Edit** menu, click **Fill Layer**, and select **Foreground** in the **Use** box and click **OK**.

STEP 6 Change the color of the lower right mat to **pea green**. Remember to lock each layer's transparent pixels before filling with color.

STEP 7 Change the color of the top left mat to **red**.

STEP 8 Change the color of the vellum layer to **light teal** and raise its opacity to **40%**.

STEP 9 Change the color of the journaling box to **light teal**. **④**

STEP 10 Now you're going to add an overlay pattern

ⓘ **TECH TIP**

Here's a shortcut for filling image layers quickly with foreground and background colors without having to first lock their transparent pixels. Press **SHIFT+ALT+DELETE** to fill the non-transparent pixels of a layer with the foreground color. Press **SHIFT+CTRL+DELETE** (**SHIFT+CMD+DELETE** on a Mac) to fill them with the background color.

to your page background. First, open the Sedona overlay file *sdovrly1.png* from the sdelements folder in the Sedona Collection on the CD.

Each collection on the *Digital Designs for Scrapbooking* CD contains a page overlay file that is designed to be used with solid backgrounds. These overlays allow you to create your own custom backgrounds.

STEP 11 Select the journaling layer, then copy and paste the entire overlay file onto your page. It should be just above your journaling layer in the **Layers** palette. Rename this layer *overlay*. (Don't worry, you'll trim away most of this.) **⑤**

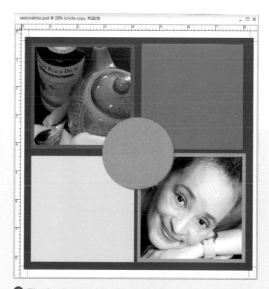

④ *The background, mats, and vellum layers have all been added.*

ⓘ **DESIGN TIP**

I like the look of mixed patterns in layouts. However, I know how easy it is to overwhelm a page or create pattern conflict instead of pattern harmony! That's why I designed the Sedona Collection's backgrounds to work together, so you can safely mix them within your page layouts.

STEP 12 If you haven't already, turn on your rulers and adjust the zero origin point.

STEP 13 Now you'll select the portions of the overlay that you want to keep. Using the **Rectangular Marquee** tool, drag a selection marquee beginning at **4"** on the horizontal ruler at any point inside the **white** crop area at the top of the page. Continue dragging until you reach the top of the **green** mat and anywhere inside the **white** crop area on the right. Zoom in to this area if you need to. ❻

STEP 14 Add the area behind the journaling block to the selection marquee.

In the **Marquee** tool options bar, click the **Add to Selection** button. ❼ Notice that the crosshairs on the **Marquee** tool's pointer now have a small **+** sign added. Whatever you select will now be added to your previous selection.

Begin dragging the pointer at the lower left corner of the existing selection ❽ and continue until the pointer is anywhere inside the crop areas to the left and at the bottom of your scrapbook page. These two selections represent the part of the overlay we're going to preserve. We'll remove the rest. ❾

❶ TECH TIP

If you have trouble with this step or find you've added an ellipse instead of a rectangle to your original selection, don't panic. From the **Edit** menu, click **Undo** to undo your last action.

❼ *The **Add to Selection** button on the **Marquee** tool options bar.*

❺ *Paste the overlay on your page.*

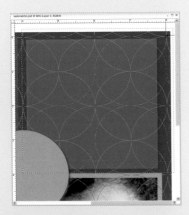

❻ *The upper right corner of the page is selected with the **Rectangular Marquee**.*

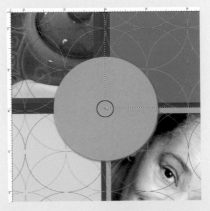

❽ *The starting point for the second selection.*

Whenever you want to remove everything *except* the area you have selected, simply choose the inverse of your selection. From the **Select** menu, click **Inverse**.

STEP 15 Make sure the overlay layer is selected, then from the **Select** menu, click **Inverse**.

STEP 16 From the **Edit** menu, click **Delete** to remove the inverted selection area (the area outside your original marquee selections). ⑩

If the overlay still extends a bit into the **pea green** mat area, don't worry. Just hold down the **CTRL** key (**CMD** on a Mac) and click inside the mat's thumbnail in the **Layers** palette. With the overlay layer selected, open the **Edit** menu and click **Delete**. This will eliminate any stray part of the overlay from the mat area.

STEP 17 To turn off the selection marquee, either open the **Select** menu and click **Deselect**, or press **CTRL** (**CMD** on a Mac) and type the **D** key. Then, click the **New Selection** button in the marquee's options bar, so that it won't try to add selections together next time you use the **Rectangular Marquee** tool.

STEP 18 To add a pattern to the circle in the middle, open the *sdbgrnd1b.jpg* file from the sdbackgrounds folder in the Sedona Collection on the CD.

The circle is the focal point of the title page, so let's dress it up a bit.

STEP 19 Select the circle layer. Then hold the **CTRL** key (**CMD** on a Mac) and click its thumbnail.

STEP 20 Using any **Marquee** tool, drag the selection marquee to the background file's window. Position it over the area you want to copy, then copy and paste it onto your scrapbook page. ⑪

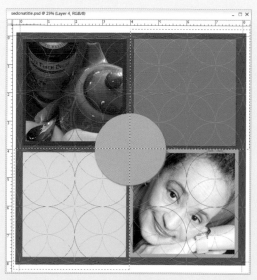

⑨ *Both selections are added together.*

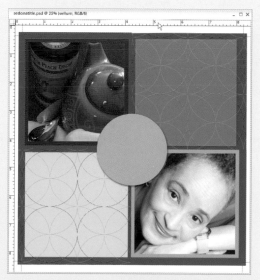

⑩ *Unwanted portions of the overlay have been removed.*

STEP 21 Rotate the pattern. Select the **Move** tool and make sure the **Show Bounding Box** button is selected in the options bar. ⑫ Now move the cursor just outside the circle's bounding box and notice the cursor becomes a curved double-arrow. Click and drag the double-arrow around the pattern circle until you're satisfied with the rotation. ⑬

STEP 22 Merge the placeholder layer with the new pattern circle layer so that the pattern circle layer will inherit the placeholder's drop shadow.

First, make sure the circle pattern layer is selected, then click the **Link** icon next to the circle placeholder layer. Then from the **Layers** menu, click **Merge Linked**.

STEP 23 To add a large bookplate open the *sdbkplts.png* file from the sdelements folder in the Sedona Collection on the CD.

Use the **Rectangular Marquee** tool to select one of

the bookplates (the example uses the large **dark teal** one). Copy and paste it onto your scrapbook page, above the pattern circle layer.

STEP 24 To add a large tab open the *sdtabs.png* file from the sdelements folder in the Sedona Collection on the CD.

Copy and paste one of the large tabs (the example uses the **red** one) onto your scrapbook page, above the pattern circle layer and below the bookplate layer. Resize the tab so it fits neatly behind the bookplate.

STEP 25 To add two small brads open the *sdbrads.png* file from the same sdelements folder.

⑫ *The* **Move** *tool options bar.*

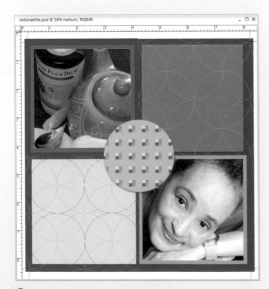

⑪ *A pattern background has been pasted onto the circle.*

⑬ *The rotated circle and bounding box.*

Copy and paste one of the brads (I used the small **light teal** brad) onto your scrapbook page. Then paste another copy of the same brad. Now position your brads above the bookplate layer to cover the holes.

STEP 26 So your journaling won't be difficult to read, reduce the opacity of the overlay area covering the journaling block by making that section of overlay its own layer.

Hold down **CTRL** (**CMD** on a Mac) and click the journaling layer's thumbnail. Make sure the overlay layer is selected. From the **Edit** menu, click **Cut**.

Hold down **CTRL** (**CMD**) and click the journaling layer thumbnail again. From the **Edit** menu, click **Paste**. Now that portion of the overlay is on its own layer and you can lower the opacity to **20%**. ⓮

STEP 27 Now add a title, journaling, and any other elements you'd like to your page.⓯

STEP 28 Save your file.

Congratulations! You've created your own Simple Scheme and made a scrapbook page from it. Now, complete this album by using the following matching schemes from the Schemes folder on the CD

81schmded.psd–Dedication

81schmtoc.psd–Table of Contents

81schmsec.psd–Section

81schmfil1.psd–Filler 1

81schmfil2.psd–Filler 2

In the next chapter you'll learn some of my favorite Photoshop Elements tips and techniques.

⓯ *The completed page.*

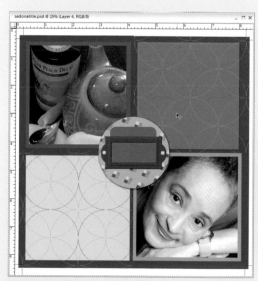

⓮ *Bookplate, tab, and brad elements have been added to the page.*

🛈 **DESIGN TIP**

My example uses the following fonts, but you can use any font you prefer

Pleasures - Adobe Caslon Pro (Italic)

Simple – Adobe Caslon Pro (Regular)

Journaling - Comic Sans

73

sweet success

title page

pleasures

simple

a cup of ginger peach tea
holding kurt's hand · foot rubs

pleasures

being silly · laughing hard while being silly
dancing · singing · moonlit dinners · warm hugs
audiobooks · real books · real simple magazine
nipping with my cats · shake it 'til · daydreaming
hearing snowrope tumble across the phone line
being a grandma · playing scrabble with kurt
long baths · being happy just being me

dedication page

Be content with what you have, rejoice in the way
things are. When you realize there is nothing
lacking, the whole world belongs to you.

Lao Tzu

July 2005   *pleasures*

table of contents

pleasures

simple

soul

mind

heart

body

section page

body

There must be quite a few things a hot bath won't
cure, but I don't know many of them
Sylvia Plath

filler spread left page

body

A crust eaten in peace is better
than a banquet partaken in anxiety
Lao Tzu

filler spread right page

When I am attacked by gloomy
thoughts, nothing helps me so much
as running to my books They quicky
absorb me and banish the clouds
from my mind. ● *Michel de Montaigne*

mind

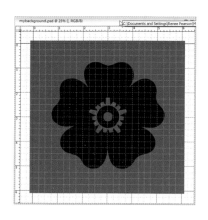

my favorite tips and techniques

Welcome to my digital studio! Here's where I'll share some of my favorite techniques—techniques I used to create the backgrounds and elements on the *Digital Designs for Scrapbooking* CD. I'll reveal secrets for creating quick yet stunning backgrounds and show you how to customize some of the elements to give them your own personalized look.

In this chapter, you'll use the Greenwich Collection. This is probably my favorite collection because of its elegance. It's ideal for heritage albums and wedding gift albums, and the colors are perfect for Christmas albums, too.

In this chapter, you'll learn how to:

- Use type as a decorative element in a background
- Apply advanced layering techniques
- Modify elements to enhance your designs
- Combine the techniques to create an elegant wedding album

Collection: Greenwich
Page size: 6" x 6"

the power of type

Type—it's not just for titles and journaling anymore! Did you know picture fonts, sometimes called dingbats, can be a wonderful source for background images?

In this lesson, you'll explore just how versatile type can be by creating a subtly elegant background page.

OBJECTIVES

- Create a font sample page
- Use the **Paint Bucket** tool
- Enlarge type
- Use blending modes
- Duplicate a layer
- Lock layers
- Use filters

STEP 1 Create a new file to store your type symbols in. You'll use this file as a sample page you can refer to when using picture fonts. We'll call this your "font sample page." (If you already have a font organizer program on your computer that allows you to cut and paste, you can skip this step.)

From the **File** menu, point to **New**, then click **Blank File**. The **New** dialog box will appear. In the **Name** box, type *picfont*. From the **Preset** list, click **Letter**. In the **Resolution box**, type **72** and leave its units as **pixels/inch**. Leave the **Background Contents** as **white**. Then click **OK**. ❶

STEP 2 Select the **Horizontal Type** tool, then specify a picture font and font size in the options bar. The example uses the **Wingding** font in **48 point** size.

STEP 3 Type every letter, number, and special character on your keyboard. Some fonts have different symbols for uppercase letters, so remember to type all the characters once in lowercase, and once with **CAPS LOCK** turned on. ❷

Because Photoshop Elements doesn't automatically wrap text when you're typing, you'll have to make hard returns at the end of each line of type.

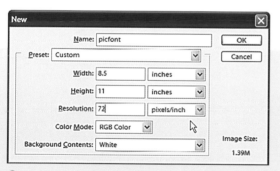

❶ *The new dialog box appears when you create a new file.*

❷ *A font sample package.*

STEP 4 Save your font sample page but don't close the window. You'll come back to it in a minute.

STEP 5 Now you'll create a new scrapbook background page. Open the file *6x6template.png* from the Extras folder on the CD and save it as *mybackground.psd*.

Make sure you save it as a Photoshop Elements (psd) file. (It will default to .png because the file you opened was a .png file.) ❸

STEP 6 If you like working with the grid and rulers, make sure they are turned on and that the zero origin point is set to match the cropmarks. Remember to turn on **Snap to Grid**. (You can toggle the grid and rulers off and on from the **View** menu. See Chapter 3, Lessons 1 and 2 for more help.)

STEP 7 Load the *greenwich.aco* color swatches from the Extras folder on the CD.

Open the **Color Swatches** palette by clicking **Color Swatches** in the **Window** menu. Click the **More** button on the **Color Swatches** palette, then click **Load Color Swatches**. Find and load the *greenwich.aco* swatches from the Extras folder on the CD. ❹

STEP 8 Double-click Layer 0's name in the **Layers** palette, and change its name to *cropmarks*.

STEP 9 Click the **Create a new layer** button at the top of the **Layers** palette to create a new layer and rename it *background*.

STEP 10 Drag the cropmarks layer to the top of the **Layers** palette. Remember always to keep this layer at the top.

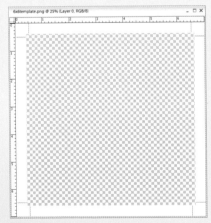

❸ The 6x6template.png *file*

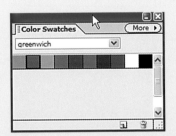

❹ The Grenwich **Color Swatches** *palette.*

ⓘ INFO TIP

As you've probably realized by now, there are often many ways to accomplish the same task in Adobe Photoshop Elements. The more familiar you become with Photoshop Elements, the more comfortable you'll become with the options available, and you'll soon settle on your favorites. In previous lessons you've learned to fill areas with color by using the **Fill Layer** and **Fill Selection** options from the **Edit** menu. This time, you'll use the **Paint Bucket** tool to fill the new background layer.

STEP 11 Select the background layer, then use the **Paint Bucket** tool to fill it with color.

In the **Color Swatches** palette, click **olive green** to load the foreground color. Then in the toolbox, click the **Paint Bucket** tool ⬧. Click anywhere inside your scrapbook page to fill the layer with **green**. ❺

STEP 12 Go back to your font sample page. Look at your samples and pick one you'd like to use as a background image. Select the **Horizontal Type** tool and click inside your sample text.

STEP 13 Highlight the picture or symbol you want to use and copy it. ❻ Go back to your background file, make sure the background layer is selected, and click anywhere in the file. Then paste the symbol onto the file. After you've pasted the symbol onto your scrapbook page, you can close the font sample file.

STEP 14 Rename the new layer *font picture*.

STEP 15 In your scrapbook page, double-click the new font picture layer's thumbnail to select the font picture (symbol).

STEP 16 Enlarge and center the font picture on the page.

In the font size box in the options bar, type **500 pt**. If that makes the picture too large, decrease the font size. If it's too small, increase it until you're satisfied with how the picture fills the page. Then click the **Move** tool and use it to center the picture in your scrapbook page. (Use the grid if you need to.) ❼

STEP 17 In the **Layers** palette, double-click the font picture's thumbnail to select it again so you can change its color.

❺ *The background layer is filled with* **olive green.**

❻ *Highlighting a font picture to copy.*

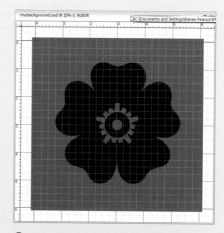

❼ *Enlarged and centered font picture.*

STEP 18 In the options bar, click the arrow next to the **Color** box, then click a color from the Greenwich collection. (The example uses **sage green**.) The font picture changes to the new font color.

STEP 19 To make the picture more subtle, reduce the font picture layer's opacity until it's barely visible. (The example uses **15%**). ❽ To reduce the opacity, select the font picture layer, click the arrow beside the **Opacity** box, and move the slider until you're satisfied.

STEP 20 Save your file. If you're happy with the new background, you can stop here.

In the next few steps you'll learn a few more techniques to make interesting backgrounds based on type.

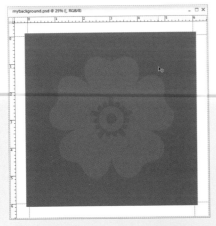

❽ *The background page with a subtle font picture.*

Use a layer blending mode

Blending modes affect how the selected layer will blend with the layers beneath it. (If you apply a blending mode to the bottom layer nothing will happen because there's no layer below it to blend with.) Using blending modes, you can create a variety of special effects. Let's practice with different blending modes to see what they can do.

First, select the font picture's layer and increase its opacity back up to **100%**. The blending mode drop-down menu is located at the top of the **Layers** palette, next to the **Opacity** box. Click the **Blending Mode** box to make the menu appear. ❾ The default mode is **Normal**, which does nothing to the layer.

Select each of the other modes in turn and notice how your font picture changes in appearance. See Adobe Photoshop Elements **Help** for a detailed explanation of each mode.

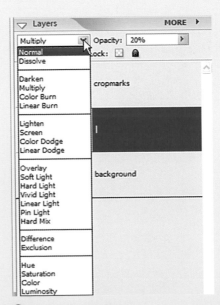

❾ *The Blending Mode menu.*

When you've tried all of the modes, select the one you prefer. (For the example, I selected the **Multiply** mode, which darkens the pixels and gives it a dramatic appeal.) If you don't like any of the blending modes, simply select **Normal** and your picture will go back to its original appearance.

Now, if you like, reduce the opacity again. ❿

SPECIAL EFFECTS TECHNIQUE 2

Apply a filter

Filters change the way your images look by applying different effects to them. Filters are one of the most powerful features in Photoshop Elements.

You've already used one of the filters—the **Gaussian Blur** filter, which you applied in Chapter 3, lesson 2. There are several more types of filters that can change

your image in many ways, from smudging out small imperfections to changing the lighting to making your photograph look like a fine art painting complete with brush strokes. To learn more about filters, see Adobe Photoshop Elements **Help.**

Filters are different from blending modes. A filter affects a single layer (or selected portion of a layer), rather than blending pixels from multiple layers. You can add multiple filters to one or more layers, and you can even blend those layers and filters together using blending modes.

Another important difference is that once you commit to a filter you cannot change it back to "normal." Because of this, always duplicate the layer you're applying the filter to and experiment with the duplicated layer.

Let's try using a filter:

Select the font picture layer, then from the **Layer** menu, click **Duplicate Layer**. ⓫

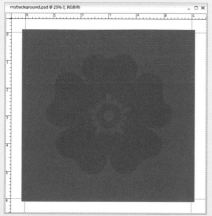

❿ *The picture font has been modified by applying the* ***Multiply*** *blending mode.*

⓫ *A font layer is duplicated in the* ***Layers*** *palette.*

To make sure you don't accidentally change your original layer, lock all of its pixels (not just the transparent pixels). To lock the pixels, select the original layer, then click the **Lock all** button at the top of the **Layers** palette. (The **Lock all** button is shaped like a padlock.) ⑫

Next, to keep from being confused by the original layer, turn off its visibility by clicking the eye icon beside the original layer's thumbnail. Now you can work with your duplicated layer.

First, select the duplicated layer and reset it to **Normal** blending mode and return its opacity to **100%**.

Before you can apply a filter to a type layer, you must simplify it. From the **Layer** menu, click **Simplify Layer**.

Open the **Filter** menu to see the available filter categories. As you move down the list, you can see the variety of options available for each filter category.

From the **Filter** menu, point to **Artistic**, and click one of the filters. A dialog box will appear with options for

that filter, a gallery of thumbnails for all the filters in the **Artistic** filter category, and a preview window. ⑬ Spend some time playing with the filter settings, and adjust the intensity of each setting using the sliders. Notice that a layer for the filter is listed in the bottom right corner of the dialog box.

Choose other filters from the open dialog box. As you select a filter, that filter replaces the previous one in the layer list.

If you want to try applying more than one filter to a layer for an interesting effect, click the **New Effect Layer** button at the bottom of the dialog box, just beneath the list of filter layers. Now when you select a new filter, that filter will be added to the list of layers, instead of replacing the previous one.

Don't forget to try filters from other filter categories, too. The example uses the **Craquelure** filter from the **Texture** filter category. ⑭

⑫ The *Lock all* button on the *Layers* palette.

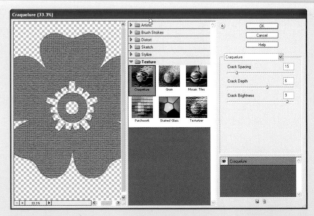

⑬ The *Filter* dialog box shows available filters and options in the *Artistic* category.

Combine filters with blending mode

Now that you know how blending modes work and how filters work, you can achieve even more interesting effects by combining the two.

Using the layer you applied a filter to, try changing the blending mode until you're satisfied.

Finally, reduce the opacity if appropriate. In the example, I applied the **Craquelure** filter, then added the **Multiply** blending mode to the same layer. Finally, I changed the layer's opacity to **30%**. Sometimes just a subtle texture is all you need. ⓯

When you've selected the filters and blending modes you want to use, and you're satisfied with the way your font picture looks, you can delete the original font picture layer and just keep the modified duplicate layer. If you don't like any of the filters or blending

modes you applied, or want to start over, delete the duplicate layer and go back to the original layer.

When you're finished with the layers, save your file.

And there you have it! You've created a simple page background using type. You can continue to add symbols to the page or leave it as it is. The design choice is yours.

Now, create a scrapbook page using your new background.

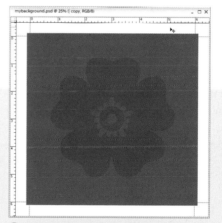

⓯ The font picture with *Craquelure* filter, *Multiply* blending mode, and **30%** opacity.

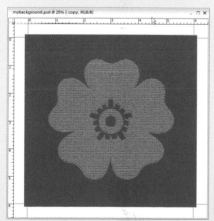

⓮ The *Craquelure* filter from the **Texture** category has been applied to the font picture.

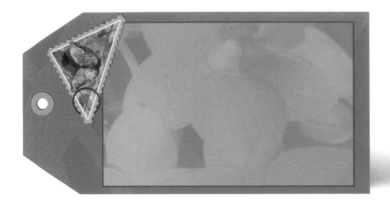

using layering techniques to customize embellishments

The *Digital Designs for Scrapbooking* CD contains many elements you can use in your scrapbooks. But don't stop there! By layering and modifying different elements in the collections, you can create an endless array of your own custom embellishments.

In this lesson on layering techniques, you'll actually do two different exercises. The first exercise will walk you through concealing and revealing portions of elements, so that it appears that one element is inside of another. The second lesson will explain how to create and use a mask layer.

OBJECTIVES

- Conceal portions of a layer
- Use the **Eraser** tool
- Use **Stroke (Outline)**
- Use **Free Transform**
- Create a mask layer

In this lesson, you'll be using many of the techniques you've already learned. If you need a refresher with any steps that aren't explained here, refer to the previous chapters for how-to details.

concealing and revealing portions of an element.

In a paper scrapbook, it's an easy thing to insert an embellishment inside another. To do the same thing in Adobe Photoshop Elements takes a little finesse. We'll use this technique to embellish one of the tags from the Greenwich collection. Here's how:

STEP 1 Open the *grtags.png* file from the grelements folder in the Greenwich Collection on the CD.

STEP 2 Use the **Rectangular Marquee** tool to select one of the blank rectangular tags and copy it.

STEP 3 Close the *grtags.png* file.

STEP 4 Open a new blank file.

Because you copied the tag, the **New** dialog box retains the dimensions and resolution of your tag. For the **Background Contents**, select **Transparent**.

STEP 5 Name your new file *mytag* and click **OK**. At this point, you've created a new file and named it, but you haven't really saved it. To save it, open the **File** menu and click **Save As**, then name it *mytag.psd*.

STEP 6 Paste the tag into the new file. ❶ Name this layer *tag*.

STEP 7 Open the *grstamps.png* file from the same folder on the CD, select a stamp and copy it onto your tag. Rename this layer *stamp*. Close the *grstamps.png* file.

STEP 8 Open the *grconchos.png* file, select a concho and copy it onto your tag. Rename this layer *concho*. Then close the *grconchos.png* file.

STEP 9 Arrange your layers so the concho layer is at the top of the stack. ❷

❶ *The new file with the tag copied into it.*

❷ *The stamp and cnocho are copied into the new file.*

STEP 10 Use the **Move** tool to position the concho over the bottom left corner of the stamp. (Zoom in on the stamp if necessary to see it more clearly.) ❸

Now that the concho is in position, you can see that you need to remove a part of the concho to create the illusion that the corner of the stamp is inserted through it.

STEP 11 Because it's easy to make a mistake when you're erasing part of an element, let's make a duplicate of the concho layer and work with the duplicate layer instead of the original.

Select the concho layer and then from the **Layer** menu, click **Duplicate Layer**. On the original concho layer, click the **Lock All** button in the **Layers** palette. Finally, click the **Eye** icon to turn off the original layer's visibility. Now we can't see the layer, but it's still there if we need to go back to it.

STEP 12 Select the **Eraser** tool ✐. In the options bar, click the arrow next to the brush sample to see the **Brushes** list. If you click the **Brushes** list, a drop-down menu will display brush categories. Select **Default Brushes**. Now scroll the mouse down across the list of brush settings to see each setting's name and size. Select the brush labeled **Hard round 13 pixels**. Make sure **Opacity** is set to **100%**. ❹

STEP 13 Carefully erase the portions of the concho you want to appear "behind" the stamp by slowly clicking over the parts you want to erase.

Don't click and drag. While this will work, you'll be more prone to accidentally erasing portions you want to keep. By using clicks, you can evaluate your progress after each click.

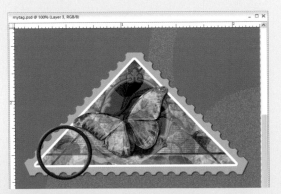
❸ *The concho is in position over the stamp.*

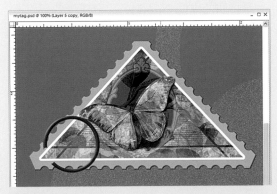
❺ *Partially erased concho.*

❹ *The **Eraser Tool** options bar*

Start with the easiest, most obvious areas first, saving the areas where the concho comes into contact with the edges of the stamp for last. ❺

Zoom in extremely close for more accuracy. You may want to reduce the size of the brush as you carefully erase the edges of the concho where it meets the stamp. ❻

To reduce the brush size, go back to the **Eraser** tool options bar, click the arrow next to the **Size** box and use the slider to change the size of the brush.

If you find you've erased a portion you needed to keep, simply use **Undo** to reverse the step.

Remember, you can always discard the layer and start over by duplicating your original concho layer.

STEP 14 Zoom out to see your entire stamp again. You did it! If you're satisfied with your erasures, unlock

and delete the original concho layer.

STEP 15 Link the concho layer to the stamp layer so you can move them together on the tag. Select the concho layer and click the **Link** icon next to the stamp thumbnail in the **Layers** palette.

STEP 16 Select the **Move** tool, and make sure **Show Bounding Box** in the options bar is selected. Then rotate or resize the linked stamp and concho to suit your taste. ❼

STEP 17 If you want more depth, add a shadow to your stamp layer.

STEP 18 Save your file, but don't close it. You'll be using it in the next exercise.

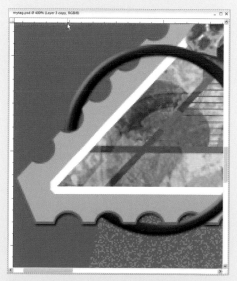

❻ 400% zoom, showing edges carefully erased.

❼ The finished stamp and concho.

creating and using a mask layer.

One of the integral features of the full-featured Adobe Photoshop program that's not available in Adobe Photoshop Elements is the Layer Mask. Masks control how different areas within a layer are hidden and revealed. By making changes to the mask, you can apply a variety of changes to the layer without actually affecting the pixels on that layer.

While you can't create integrated layer masks in Photoshop Elements, I'll show you how to create your own mask layers and how to use them. The type of mask layer you'll create has a shape cut out of it that is the exact size and shape of the photo or element you want to use. You use the mask layer as a frame or reverse stencil—you can see the portion of a photo through the cut-out hole in the mask layer, so that you know just which part of the photo to use.

We'll continue to work with the tag by adding a journaling area with a faded photo background.

STEP 1 Turn off the visibility of the stamp and concho layers by clicking their **Eye** icons.

STEP 2 Create a new layer named *journaling* just above the bottom layer.

STEP 3 Using whichever method you prefer (creating a shape layer or using the **Rectangular Marquee** tool) create a journaling block area and fill it with color from the *greenwich.aco* swatch palette. (The example uses the **yellow** color swatch.) ❶

STEP 4 Now you'll add a slim border around the block in a different color. First, create a new layer just above the journaling layer, and name the new layer *border*.

❶ *A **yellow** journaling block is added to the tag.*

By adding the border on a separate layer, you can change its color and make other adjustments without altering the journaling block.

STEP 5 Click one of the darker colors from the **Color Swatches** palette. This loads the foreground color with the new border color.

STEP 6 Hold down **CTRL** (**CMD** on a Mac) and click the journaling block's thumbnail in the **Layers** palette.

STEP 7 Select the border layer, then from the **Edit** menu click **Stroke (Outline) Selection**. The **Stroke** dialog box appears. ❷

Set the **Width** to **6 pixels** (increase the size if you want a wider border), and set the **Location** to **Center** (which centers the border over the selection marquee). Leave the **Blending Mode** set to **Normal** and the **Opacity** set at **100%**. Then click **OK**. ❸

STEP 8 Turn off the selection marquee by clicking **Deselect** from the **Select** menu.

STEP 9 Choose a photo you want to use as a subtle background for your journaling block. Open the photo, and copy and paste it onto your tag.

STEP 10 Make sure this new photo layer is above the journaling layer. ❹

STEP 11 Hold down **CTRL** (**CMD** on a Mac) and click the journaling block's thumbnail in the **Layers** palette. The selection marquee appears, outlining the shape of the journaling block even though the journaling block is hidden behind your photo.

STEP 12 Create a new layer above the photo layer and name it *mask*. This is the layer you'll use to determine how to resize and crop the photo to fit your area.

STEP 13 From the **Select** menu, click **Inverse**. Now

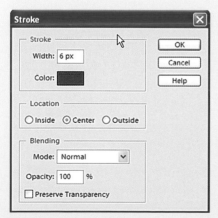

❷ The *Stroke* dialog box.

❸ The tag now has a journaling box and border.

❹ A photo has been added to the tag.

the area outside the journaling block will be selected.

STEP 14 Fill the inverted selection with **black**. To do this, click **black** in the **Color Swatches** palette, then select the **Paint Bucket** tool and click in the image. The area you can now see through is the exact size you need for your photo. ❺

STEP 15 Lock the mask layer by selecting it and clicking the **Lock all** button. You don't want to accidentally change the mask layer because you'll use it as a window as you resize and move the photo around.

STEP 16 Now it's time to resize and crop your photo. Although you can use the **Move** tool (with **Show Bounding Box** turned on) to resize and move the photo around behind the mask until it's positioned the way you want it, we're going to use another feature called **Free Transform**, to modify the photo. Select the photo layer, then from the **Image** menu, point to **Transform**, then click **Free Transform**. A bounding box with handles appears around your photo.

STEP 17 Move the photo around until the image inside the mask's window is positioned where you want it. To resize the photo, hold down **SHIFT** (or click the **Maintain aspect ratio button** in the options bar) then move a corner handle. If your photo is larger than the document window itself, you may not see the bounding box and its corners. Enlarge the entire document window (not the image or the mask) by dragging a corner of the window until you can see the photo's bounding box. When you're done press the **ENTER** key, and the transformation will take effect. ❻

STEP 18 Turn off the mask layer's visibility.

STEP 19 Hold down **CTRL** (**CMD** on a Mac) and click the mask layer's thumbnail in the **Layers** palette.

❺ The mask layer has a window the exact size of the jorunaling block.

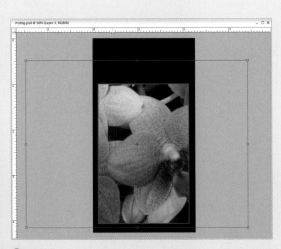

❻ The mask window shows the resized and repositioned photo behind it.

ⓘ INFO TIP

Free Transform is probably the feature I use most frequently in Photoshop Elements. With this feature, I can experiment with moving, rotating, skewing, distorting, resizing, and changing the perspective of a layer. I don't have to use a different command for each action—I can use **Free Transform** to make several changes at once, and the changes aren't committed until I hit the **ENTER** key or switch to a different tool. For more information about **Free Transform**, see Adobe Photoshop Elements **Help.**

STEP 20 Select the photo layer, then press **Delete**. This will remove the portion of the photo that was outside the mask's window.

STEP 21 From the **Select** menu, click **Deselect** to turn off the selection marquee.

STEP 22 If your photo was larger than your tag, there may still be portions of the photo outside the image window. To remove any excess, first choose **All** from the **Select** menu. Then, from the **Image** menu, click **Crop**.

STEP 23 Now reduce the photo layer's opacity so your photo serves as a subtle background for your journaling area. ❼

STEP 24 Turn on the vIsIbility of the stamp and concho layers. Link and reposition them if necessary.

STEP 25 Save your finished tag as a .png file. From the **File** menu, click **Save As**, and name it *mytag.png*. Select the **PNG** file format, then click **OK**. ❽ When asked if you want to save the file as **Interlaced** or with **None**, select **Interlaced**, the default. If you think you'll want to make more adjustments to your tag's design, save it also as a .psd file.

Now you can use this tag in your scrapbook layouts!

Continue to experiment with layering and masks to create more custom elements for your scrapbooking projects.

❼ *The photo has been resized and cropped, and its opacity has been reduced.*

❽ *The finished tag.*

ℹ **DESIGN TIP**

Reducing the opacity of photos and backgrounds is an amazingly simple way to create elegant backdrops that are perfect for wedding and heritage scrapbook pages. Floral photos are perfect for this technique, so take lots of close-up pictures in your garden to have on hand.

ℹ **TECH TIP**

PNG (Portable Network Graphics) files save transparent backgrounds without jagged edges. Because we want to preserve the transparency around the tag and inside its "hole" for future use in layouts, be sure you save your tag in the PNG file format.

modifying the elements

You've learned how to create stunning page layouts using the elements from the *Digital Designs for Scrapbooking* CD. Now let's talk about how to modify those elements.

Some of the elements lend themselves to modification more than others. The postage stamps are a good example of elements that are easy to modify. Let's begin there.

In this lesson, there are two exercises. In the first one, you'll customize a postage stamp. In the second one, you'll learn how to enlarge an image without degrading its quality.

OBJECTIVES

- Use the **Magic Wand** tool
- Enlarge images with the **Bicubic Smoother** option
- Sharpen images with a **Sharpen** filter

Remember, if you need help with any of the steps not explained fully in this lesson, refer to the previous chapters for more detailed instructions.

customize a postage stamp.

Each of the collections on the *Digital Designs for Scrapbooking* CD contains a set of postage stamps. In this exercise you'll recolor a stamp and add a decorative background.

STEP 1 Open the *grstamps.png* file from the grelements folder in the CD's Greenwich Collection.

STEP 2 Use the **Rectangular Marquee** tool to select one of the solid color stamps and copy it.

STEP 3 Close the *grstamps.png* file.

STEP 4 Open a new blank file.

Because you copied the stamp onto the clipboard, the **New** dialog box retains the dimensions and resolution of your tag. For the **Background Contents**, select **Transparent**.

STEP 5 Name your new file *mystamp* and click **OK**. At this point, you've created a new file and named it, but you haven't really saved it. To save it, open the **File menu** and click **Save As**, then name it *mystamp.psd*.

STEP 6 Paste the stamp into the new window. ❶ Name this layer *stamp*.

STEP 7 The stamps in this collection all have a **sage green** frame around them. Let's change that to **white**. First, create a new layer and name it *frame*.

STEP 8 Select the **Magic Wand** tool from the toolbox. In the options bar, set the **Tolerance** at **2.** Make sure the **Anti-aliased** and **Contiguous** buttons are checked.

STEP 9 Select the original stamp layer and click the **Lock all** button so you won't accidentally change it.

STEP 10 With the **Magic Wand** tool, click anywhere

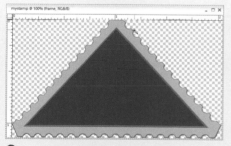

❶ *The new file with the stamp copied into it.*

ⓘ INFO TIP

The **Magic Wand** tool selects pixels within a color range. It's great for selecting solid color areas. To learn more about the **Magic Wand** tool and **Tolerance** settings, see Adobe Photoshop Elements **Help.**

inside the frame area of the original stamp. This will draw a selection marquee around the stamp's frame.

STEP 11 Select the *frame* layer.

STEP 12 Click the **white** swatch in the **Color Swatches** palette, then select the **Paint Bucket** tool and click inside the marqee to fill the frame with **white**. ❷

STEP 13 Turn off the selection marquee.

Next, you'll replace the inside area of the stamp with a decorative background. To do this, you can use either of the methods you've learned so far. The first method is to click inside the stamp's solid area with the **Magic Wand** tool, then use one of the **Marquee** tools to drag the selection marquee to a background image and copy and paste it into place between the stamp layer and the frame layer.

The second method is to use a mask layer so that you can resize the background after you've copied it into your stamp image. Let's use the mask layer method for this exercise

STEP 14 Open the image you want to use as a background for your stamp, copy a portion of it, and paste it onto your stamp. The example uses one of the Greenwich backgrounds. ❸

STEP 15 Select the stamp layer, then use the **Magic Wand** tool and click inside the stamp's solid area. (Even though you can't see the stamp, you know where it's solid area should be, so click in that area.) The selection marquee appears, outlining the stamp's solid area even though it's still hidden behind your background image.

STEP 16 Create a new layer above the background image layer and name it *mask*.

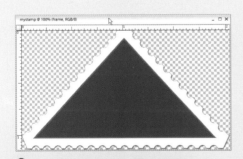

❷ The stamp now has a **white** frame.

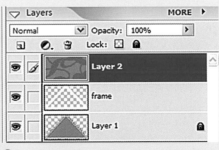

❸ Background from the Greenwich collection.

STEP 17 From the **Select** menu, click **Inverse**. Now the area outside the stamp's center will be selected.

STEP 18 Click black in the **Color Swatches** palette, then select the **Paint Bucket** tool and click inside the marquee. ❹

STEP 19 Lock the mask layer by selecting it and clicking the **Lock all** button.

STEP 20 Select the background image layer, then use either the **Move** tool or the **Free Transform** feature to resize and position your background image.

STEP 22 Turn off the mask layer's visibility.

STEP 23 Hold down **CTRL** (**CMD** on a Mac) and click the mask layer's thumbnail in the **Layers** palette.

STEP 24 Select the background image layer, then press **Delete**. This will remove the portion of the photo

that was outside the mask's window.

STEP 25 From the **Select** menu, click **Deselect** to turn off the selection marquee.

STEP 26 If your background image was larger than your stamp, there may still be portions of the photo outside the image window. To remove any excess, choose **All** from the **Select** menu. Then, from the **Image** menu, click **Crop**. ❺

STEP 27 Now you can change the color of the narrow border just inside the frame. First, create a new layer and name it *border*.

STEP 28 Select the **Magic Wand** tool.

STEP 29 Select the original stamp layer, and with the **Magic Wand** tool, click anywhere inside the border area of the original stamp. This will draw a selection marquee around the stamp's inside border. (You may

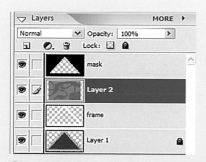

❹ The *Layers* palette shows the mask layer.

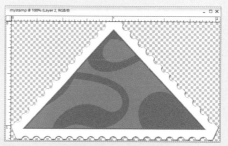

❺ The stamp has a new background.

need to zoom in on the stamp to see the border more clearly.)

STEP 30 Select the border layer.

STEP 31 Click a color in the **Color Swatches** palette, then select the **Paint Bucket** tool and click anywhere inside the marquee to fill the border with that color.

STEP 32 Turn off the selection marquee. ❻

STEP 33 For fun, add some text.

STEP 34 When you are sure you're finished with your stamp, you can delete the mask layer and merge the rest of the layers. To merge layers, select one of the layers and then click the link icon beside all the remaining layers. Then, from the **Layer** menu, click **Merge Linked**.

ⓘ **INFO TIP**

Merging the layers reduces the size of the file. You won't be able to edit the individual layers anymore, but that's okay, because now you know how easy it is to start with one of the stamps from the *grstamps.png* file and create a brand new one!

STEP 35 Now save the file as a .png file. ❼ Saving it as a .png file will enable you to copy this stamp and paste it onto your future scrapbook pages.

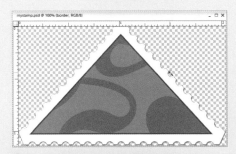
❻ *All areas of the stamp have been replaced.*

❼ *The completed stamp.*

enlarging images.

Occasionally you may want to enlarge an element beyond its original size. However, simply enlarging elements and photos will give them a pixelated quality.

Fortunately, Photoshop Elements includes two features that will help preserve the quality of your images after you enlarge them. This exercise will show you how.

STEP 1 Open the *grconchos.png* file from the grelements folder in the Greenwich collection on the CD, and select and copy one of the conchos.

STEP 2 Create a new file and name it *bigconcho*. Select **white** as the **Background Contents**.

STEP 3 Paste the selected concho into this new window. ❶

You now have a nice, crisp image—but it's smaller than we want.

STEP 4 Enlarge the image to see how it grows pixelated and out of focus when you use Photoshop Elements' default enlargement setting (called **Bicubic**). From the **Image** menu, point to **Resize**, then click **Image Size**. In the **Document Size Width** box, type **2 inches** (the height box will change automatically). Keep the rest of the default settings as they are. Click **OK**. Notice how fuzzy the image is. ❷

STEP 5 Now, back up (using **Undo**) and do it again using the **Bicubic Smoother** setting. Again, from the **Image** menu, point to **Resize,** then click **Image Size.** In the **Document Size Width** box, type **2 inches.** Click the arrow beside the **Resample Image** box and select **Bicubic Smoother**. ❸ Keep the rest of the default settings as they are. Click **OK**.

While somewhat improved, the image is still too fuzzy. You'll take care of that in the next step by using a **Sharpen** filter.

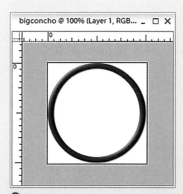

❶ *Small concho image.*

❷ *The enlarged image is out of focus.*

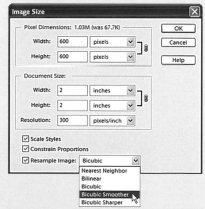

❸ *The Image Size dialog box*

STEP 6 To sharpen the image, first make sure the concho layer is selected. Then, from the **Filter** menu, point to **Sharpen**, then click **Unsharp Mask**.

STEP 7 If you can't see the edge of the concho in the dialog box window, click an edge of the concho inside the actual image window. Then go back to the dialog box.

STEP 8 Adjust the sliders in the dialog box until you're satisfied with the sharpness, then click **OK**.

As you move the sliders, watch the image sharpen inside the small window. You can also observe your image window as you make adjustments. To see just how much sharpening you've done, click the **Preview** button on and off and notice the concho in the image window change. ❹ To sharpen the concho in the example, I used **150%** for the **Amount**, and set the **Radius** to **6 pixels**. ❺

❶ **INFO TIP**

In Adobe Photoshop Elements, our resizing exercise is considered resampling because we're actually adding pixels to our image. The **Bicubic Smoother** option is better suited for enlarging images than the other options.To learn more about resizing and resampling images, see Adobe Photoshop Elements **Help**.

❶ **INFO TIP**

The Sharpen filters focus blurry images. The **Unsharp Mask** (which by its name sounds like the last filter you'd select), is actually the best suited for sharpening enlarged images. To learn more about the Sharpen filters, see Adobe Photoshop Elements **Help**.

STEP 9 To use this concho as a transparent image, delete the original white background layer and save the file as a .png file.

Continue to experiment with resampling and sharpening images. This technique is especially useful when enlarging photos. The options you select will differ depending on the image you're working with. You'll become more comfortable with this technique with practice.

Remember, Photoshop Elements cannot work miracles by turning tiny photos into sharp, 8 x 10 enlargements. However, you can make modest enlargements that will look just fine in your layouts.

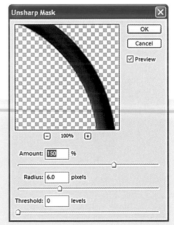

❹ *The* Unsharp mask *dialog box.*

❺ *The image of the concho has been sharpened.*

Michi & Shawn

creating an elegant wedding album

Well, here we are. It's the last lesson, and by now you've developed an impressive array of skills. You're well on your way to creating magnificent digital scrapbook pages.

In this lesson, I'll wrap up everything you've learned by showing you how I put together the pages for a beautiful 6 x 6 wedding gift album for my sister. In each exercise, I'll focus on one technique or combination of techniques you've already practiced. Here are the pages we'll create

and the techniques we'll use:

• Title and dedication pages: Embellishing type.

• Single photo page: Creating a frame.

• Bride and groom pages: Copying layers from page to page.

• Closing page: Adding a custom embellishment.

OBJECTIVES

• Embellish type
• Create shaped photo frames and mats
• Copy layers from page to page
• Add personal photos to elements

Embellishing type.

The Title Page I love designing wedding albums—they're so elegant. For the title page of this album, I've decided to use only my sister's and her husband's first names, but to embellish them so they look distinctive. ❶ Since you're so proficient with Photoshop Elements at this point, I won't detail steps you've done many times before. If you need help, review the previous chapters and lessons as refreshers.

> **ⓘ DESIGN TIP**
>
> Do your old color wedding pictures make your pages look dated? Convert them to **black** and **white** before using them. It'll give them a timeless quality.

STEP 1 Open the background image file you want to use from the Greenwich collection and save it as a .psd file.

STEP 2 Using the font and color of your choice, type the words in your page. (The example uses the Bernhard Modern font. To choose a color such as the **warm cream** color in the example, click the **Color** box in the options bar to open the **Color Picker**, then drag the white triangles along the slider, click inside the slider or click inside the color field.)

STEP 3 Duplicate the type layer twice. (From the **Layer** menu, click **Duplicate Layer**.)

STEP 4 Change the middle type layer to the darkest color you want to use. The example uses **coffee brown** from the Greenwich swatches palette. (Select the text, then click a color in the **Color Swatches** palette.)

STEP 5 Change the bottom type layer to an accent color. The example uses **yellow** from the Greenwich swatches palette.

STEP 6 Simplify the two lower layers leaving only the top layer as type. (Select a layer, then from the **Layer** menu, click **Simplify Layer**.)

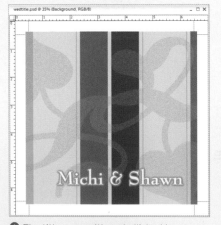

❶ *The title page with embellished type.*

❷ *The Undo History palette.*

> **ⓘ TECH TIP**
>
> The **Undo History** palette ❷ is essential when working with multiple effects and filters. The **Undo History** palette allows you to "back-up" several steps in a process. Open the **Undo History** palette from the **Window** menu by clicking **Undo History**. To learn more about the **Undo History** palette, see Adobe Photoshop Elements **Help**.

STEP 7 Turn off the top two layers' visibility and select the bottom (**yellow**) type layer.

STEP 8 Apply an **8-pixel** wide **Stroke (Outline)** to this layer using **coffee brown**. Press **CTRL** (**CMD** on a Mac) and click the layer's thumbnail. From the **Edit** menu, click **Stroke (Outline) Selection**. In the **Stroke** dialog box, type **8** in the **Width** box. Then click the **Color** box. When the **Color Picker** appears, ignore it, click **coffee brown** in the **Color Swatches** palette and click **OK**.)

STEP 9 Apply the **Gaussian Blur** filter to this layer

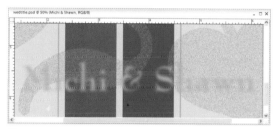

❸ *The bottom type layer with **Stroke (Outline)** and Guassian Blur filter applied.*

using a radius of **8 pixels**. (Make sure the layer is still selected, then from the **Filter** menu, point to **Blur**, then click **Gaussian Blur**. Set the **Radius** to **8 pixels**, then click **OK**. ❸

STEP 10 Now select the middle (**coffee brown**) type layer. Apply an **8-pixel** wide yellow **Stroke (Outline)** to this layer, then apply a **Gaussian Blur** filter with an **8-pixel** radius. ❹

STEP 11 To make your type "pop" from the page, duplicate the bottom type layer and the middle type layer, then offset both copies two positions to the right and two down. (To offset a layer, select it, click the **Move** tool, then press one of the **ARROW** keys to move the layer one position to the left, right, up or down.) ❺

STEP 12 Save the page as a .psd file. ❻

❹ *The middle type layer with **Stroke (Outline)** and Gaussian Blur filter applied.*

❻ *The finished page.*

❺ *The final embellished type.*

The Dedication Page This page shows another example of using type to design the entire page layout. It's a sophisticated look that only uses two very simple techniques. The hardest part of this page was selecting the right poem!

STEP 1 Open the background image file you want to use from the Greenwich collection and save it as a .psd file.

STEP 2 Using the same font you used on the title page (the example uses **Bernhard Modern** in **sage green**), type the first three words of the poem you've selected, arrange them artfully and reduce their opacity to **20%**.

STEP 3 Switching to a different font (the example uses **Zurich Extended**) in **white** and keeping it at **100%** opacity, create a new type layer and type the entire poem, giving each line its own layer. Artfully arrange the lines across the page. ❼

That's it. It's so simple, yet it looks so elegant.

Creating a frame.

Single Photo Page My favorite photo from my sister's wedding shows the two of them standing together before the minister with their heads bowed. I loved the way the candlelight is reflected in this photo and felt it deserved its own page. But what do you do to embellish a single photo page? Very little. Here's what I did. ❶

STEP 1 Open the background image file you want to use from the Greenwich collection and save it as a .psd file.

STEP 2 Copy and paste a large photo onto the page.

STEP 3 Now you're going to use the **Rounded Rectangle** shape tool to create a mask layer. First, select the **Rounded Rectangle** shape tool, and in the options bar, set the **Radius** to **40 pixels**. Draw a rectangle the size and shape you'll want your photo to fit into and position the rectangle on the page where you'll want the photo. It doesn't matter what color the rectangle is filled with. ❷

❼ *The dedication page.*

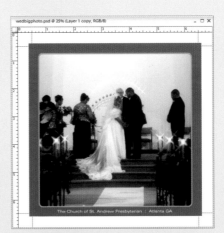

❶ *The single photo page.*

STEP 4 Create a new layer above the shape layer and name it *mask*.

STEP 5 Press **CTRL** (**CMD** on a Mac) and click the shape layer's thumbnail to select the rectangular shape.

STEP 6 Make sure the mask layer is selected, then inverse the selection and fill it with black.

STEP 7 Now you have your mask layer. Delete the rounded rectangle shape layer, because you don't need it anymore.

STEP 8 Position the photo so that the portion you want appears through the mask layer's window. ❸ Then, crop the photo to fit. (Select the photo layer, then press **CTRL** [**CMD** on a Mac] and click the mask layer's thumbnail. Turn off the mask layer's visibility. Make sure the photo layer is still selected, then press **DELETE** to crop the photo to the mask's outline. Then turn off the selection marquee.)

STEP 9 Let's add a thin border around the photo. Create a new layer above the photo layer.

STEP 10 Press **CTRL** (**CMD** on a Mac) and click the cropped photo layer's thumbnail.

STEP 11 Apply a **4-pixel** stroke to the new layer in a contrasting color. (From the **Edit** menu, click **Stroke (Outline) Selection**. In the **Stroke** dialog box, type **4** in the **Width** box. Then click the **Color** box to select a color, and click **OK**.)

STEP 12 Add the journaling in a simple font and neutral color. The example uses the **Zurich Extended** font.

STEP 13 Save the file as a .psd file.

No question, the photo is the star of this page!

❸ *Position the photo behind the mask layer.*

❷ *Use the **Rounded Rectangle** shape tool to draw a frame for the photo.*

copying a layer from one page to another.

Bride and Groom Pages You're going to love this next tip! You just spent time creating a rounded rectangle shape for the previous page. What if you'd like to use that same shape—same size, same location on the page—on another page? Sure, you could copy and paste. But what if you could just tell Photoshop Elements, "Put this in the same location on my other page." Well, you can! ❶

STEP 1 Open the background image file you want to use from the Greenwich collection and save it as a .psd file.

STEP 2 Open the single photo page from the last exercise and select the mask layer.

STEP 3 From the **Layer** menu, click **Duplicate Layer**.

STEP 4 In the **Duplicate Layer** dialog box, select the new file you just created as the **Destination**, then click

OK. ❷ Close the single photo page. The mask layer now appears in your new file. ❸

STEP 5 Copy a contrasting background and paste it into your new page between the first background layer and the mask layer. Name this new layer *mat*.

STEP 6 Use the mask to crop the new mat to the rounded rectangle shape. (Select the mat layer, then press **CTRL** (**CMD** on a Mac) and click the mask layer's thumbnail. Turn off the mask layer's visibility. Make sure the mat layer is still selected, then press **DELETE** to crop the mat to the mask's outline. Then turn off the selection marquee.)

STEP 7 Now add a thin border around the mat. (Create a new layer above the mat layer. Press **CTRL** (**CMD** on a Mac) and click the mat layer's thumbnail.

❶ The bride's page uses the same shape as the single photo page.

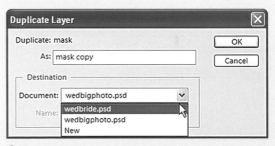

❷ The *Duplicate Layer* dialog box.

From the **Edit** menu, click **Stroke (Outline) Selection**, and apply a **4-pixel** border in a contrasting color.) ❹

Now add an oval photo to the page. While the oval photo treatment may look complex, it's actually very simple.

STEP 8 Copy and paste your photo onto the page.

STEP 9 Select the **Ellipse** shape tool and in the options bar, click the **Geometry options** arrow to select **Unconstrained** and **From Center**. (The **Unconstrained** option lets you draw an oval instead of a circle.) Create an oval shape the size you want to use for your photo. If necessary, move the new oval to the position where you want it to be on the page.

STEP 10 Now create an oval mask from the shape. (Create a new layer above the shape layer and name it *photo mask*. Press **CTRL** (**CMD** on a Mac) and click the shape layer's thumbnail. Make sure the mask layer is selected, then inverse the selection and fill it with black. Turn off the original shape layer's visibility.)

STEP 11 Select the photo layer and move it until it's centered in the mask's oval window, then crop the photo. (To crop the photo, make sure the photo layer is selected, then press **CTRL** (**CMD** on a Mac) and click the mask layer's thumbnail. Turn off the mask layer's visibility. Make sure the photo layer is still selected, then press **DELETE**. Then turn off the selection marquee.) ❺

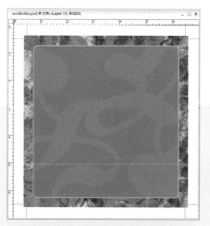

❹ *The new file has contrasting backgrounds and border.*

❺ *The photo has been cropped into an oval shape.*

❸ *The new file now contains the same mask layer.*

STEP 12 Turn on the original shape layer's visibility. You will now use this shape layer as a mat for the photo. Use any method you like to enlarge it to the size you want. Then change the color to one that matches your layout. **❻**

STEP 13 Add a **4-pixel Stroke (Outline)** around the mat and an extra-thin, **2 pixels**, one around the photo.

STEP 14 Add a drop shadow behind the mat. To change the shadow's angle and distance, double-click the small "**f**" icon beside the mat layer in the **Layers** palette. **❼**

STEP 15 Add the word "bride," reduce the text's opacity, and your layout is complete.

STEP 16 Save the file as a .psd file.

STEP 17 Now create a complementary layout for the groom page. **❽**

❻ *The shape layer has been enlarged to make it an oval mat.*

❼ *The completed photo treatment.*

❽ *The completed groom's page*

adding a custom embellishment.

Closing page Adding your own photo to one of the postage stamp elements can make a great embellishment for a scrapbook page. Even an elegant wedding page can take advantage of this technique. ❶ As you'll see, this is just a basic layering exercise with a bit of a twist.

STEP 1 Open a postage stamp file from one of the collections. Copy and paste one of the solid color stamps into a new document window.

STEP 2 Now copy and paste one of the decorative stamps into the same document. ❷

STEP 3 Create a triangle marquee by using the **Magic Wand** tool to click inside the solid center of the plain stamp.

STEP 4 Add a new layer above the decorative stamp layer and fill it with any color. This is the shape you'll use to create a mask layer for your photo.

STEP 5 Now make the inner triangle smaller so that you can see some of the decorative area from the decorative stamp. I like to use **Free Transform**, but you can use whatever technique you're comfortable with. ❸

STEP 6 Just as you've done before, use this shape to create a mask layer, then delete the original inner triangle layer.

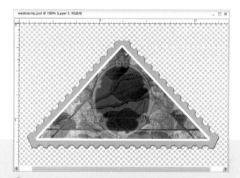

❷ A decorative stamp has been copied over a solid stamp.

❶ The closing page is embellished with a customized stamp.

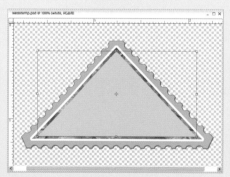

❸ You can use *Free Transform* or the *Move* tool (with *Show Bounding Box* checked) to resize the inner triangle.

STEP 7 Copy a photo onto the document, between the decorative stamp layer and the mask layer.

STEP 8 Using the mask, resize and crop your photo into the shape. Turn off the mask layer's visibility.

STEP 9 Use **Stroke (Outline)** to add a thin border around the photo and give it a polished appearance.

STEP 10 Now you can delete the solid color stamp layer and the mask layer, because you don't need them anymore.

STEP 11 Save the stamp as a .png file and use it in your layout. ❹

❹ *The finished stamp.*

this is just the beginning...

You've done it! You've created six beautiful pages, just right for a special gift album.

And now you've also finished all the lessons and exercises in this book that have to do with producing scrapbook pages. Along the way, you've created backgrounds, embellishments and mats, and you've learned ways to enhance your photos.

But now there's even more for you to explore. The *Digital Designs for Scrapbooking* CD contains a variety of templates, backgrounds and design elements that we haven't even looked at yet. Chapter 7 is a catalog of everything you can find on the CD.

If you'd like to search the CD's catalog on your computer, Photoshop Elements has a feature called the **File Browser** that lets you browse through visual files easily. To learn how to use the **File Browser,** see Adobe Photoshop Elements **Help. ❶ ❷**

As you explore the design elements on the CD and begin using them to create your own scrapbook pages, don't feel like you're restricted to using only the elements in a single collection. I designed many of the elements, such as the bookplates, buttons, brads and conchos, to be used across collections. So feel free to mix and match elements from different collections to see what new looks you can create.

In the next chapter, we'll discuss what to do with your completed projects. We'll talk about printing, trimming and sharing your digital pages.

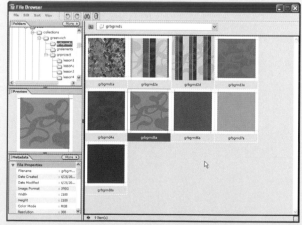

❶ *The Windows Photoshop Elements **File Browser.***

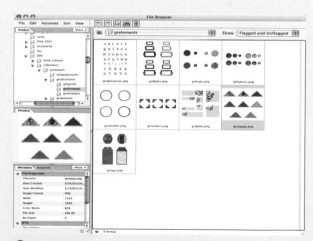

❷ *The Mac Photoshop Elements **File Browser.***

a beautiful finish

title page

Michi & Shawn

dedication page

How shall I withhold my soul
so that it does not touch yours?
How shall I uplift it over you to other things?

Ah willingly would I
by some lost thing in the dark
give it harbor in an unfamiliar silent place
that does not vibrate on when your depths vibrate.

Yet everything that touches us, you and me,
takes us together as a bow's stroke does,
that out of two strings draws a single voice.

Upon what instrument are we two spanned?
And what player has us in his hand?
Oh sweet song.   *Rainer Maria Rilke*

18 Nov 1995

photo page

The Church of St. Andrew Presbyterian : Atlanta GA

bride page

bride

groom page

groom

end page

Mr. and Mrs. Shawn Oliver

what to do with your finished pages (and other stuff)

Now that you've learned how to create great-looking pages, you may be wondering about the best way to display those pages and share them with family and friends.

The beauty of digital scrapbooking is that there are so many ways to share your pages, both in printed and digital format! In this chapter, we'll talk about a few of the more popular ways to display your carefully crafted pages. First, we'll look at printing options. Then we'll explore some digital ideas.

In this chapter:

- The printed page
- Digital albums and displays
- Resource books and websites for more information

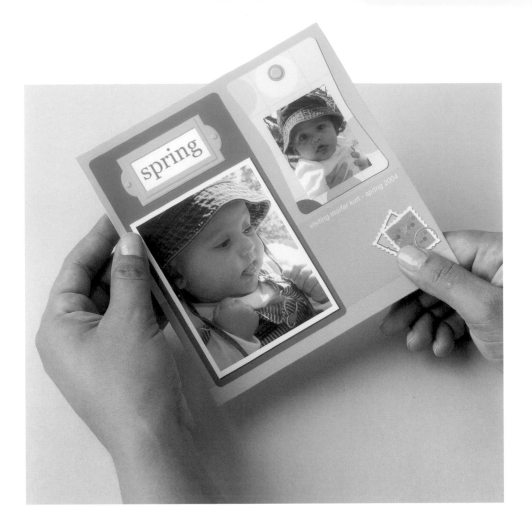

the printed page

Just because it's so easy and exciting to create digital pages doesn't mean you have to leave those pages on your computer. For many people, viewing photos on a computer screen still can't compare to flipping through pages in a beautiful album. That's why many digital scrapbookers choose to print their pages and put them in albums.

PRINTERS AND PAPERS

How well your images turn out on your home printer depends on your printer and the papers you use.

Inkjet printers seem to get better every day. Models that can print a wide range of paper sizes and resolution quality are available. I use a wide-format Epson Stylus Photo printer in my studio. This printer allows me to print pages up to 13 inches wide.

You may be surprised how much difference paper makes in your printouts. All photo papers are NOT made equal. Don't skimp on the paper for important pages.

I use Epson Professional papers for my final pages. They are more expensive, but I love the results I get. For printing backgrounds and finished page layouts, my favorite is Epson Professional Enhanced Matte. For photos I intend to print and paste onto paper layouts, I prefer Epson Professional Premium Luster.

You can find these papers at most office warehouse and computer stores, many professional camera stores, and online at websites such as inkjetart.com.

If you're on a budget, save these papers for special albums. Don't waste your "good" paper on those multiple drafts you make as you play around with your pages. Just keep in mind that the results you see on your draft paper may not match exactly the results on your "good" paper in color, brightness, bleed-through or other qualities.

ONLINE PRINTERS

If you have a regular-format printer that only can only handle up to 8½ x 11 pages, consider ordering larger pages from online resources. Some online photo processing centers, such as White House Custom Colour (whcc.com) or ScrapbookPictures.com, print and mail your oversize pages to you for a reasonable price.

ⓘ INFO TIP

A printed album is a good way to ensure your pages are preserved. Computers crash, CDs corrode in humid climates, melt in the heat or get stepped on by your visiting nephew. And, technology changes. (Remember floppy disks?) Most archivists warn against thinking of CDs as a long-term storage solution. Surprisingly, a CD's lifespan is generally considered to be decades shorter than good ol' archival paper and ink. Your best bet for a treasured album? Save your pages in both formats: make a CD, and print out your pages on archival paper. For even more security, and to protect against fire or flood, store a copy away from home.

ⓘ INFO TIP

Since I purchased my printer, Epson has introduced newer models with added features, in both wide and regular-sized format printers. If you're in the market for a new printer, list the features you want, such as page size and resolution, and look around on the internet for reviews of the newest models. For more information about Epson printers, visit epson.com.

WORKING WITH RESOLUTION

The resolution of your page makes a big difference in the quality of your printouts. Higher resolution—often referred to in dots per inch (*dpi*) for a printer, or pixels per inch (*ppi*) for a computer screen—means sharper, crisper images. Lower resolution means grainier, fuzzier images.

All of the templates, backgrounds and elements on the *Digital Designs for Scrapbooking* CD are at **300 ppi**. If you open a background or template from the CD, you will be automatically working at this resolution.

If you open a new document window in Photoshop Elements (instead of opening a background or template), you can set the resolution in the **New** dialog box. In general, it's best to set the resolution to **300 ppi**. This will ensure sharp, high-quality prints.

You can change the resolution of a page at any time from the **Image** menu by clicking **Resize**.

PRINTING OVERLAYS AND TRANSPARENCIES

Collections on the *Digital Designs for Scrapbooking* CD each contain two overlay files. These files emulate transparent overlays in the traditional scrapbooking world. Use inkjet acetate to print your overlay. This transparent film has a special coating so the ink won't smear. Purchase inkjet acetate from office supply warehouse stores such as Office Depot or Staples.

For creative and interesting effects, try printing other design elements or portions of your layout on acetate. Or, print everything except the photos on regular paper, then print the photos on acetate. Experiment!

MIXING DIGITAL AND TRADITIONAL ELEMENTS

Who says you can't mix digital and traditional elements on a scrapbook page? Sometimes, the most creative looks can come from combining the best of both the digital and the paper worlds. In fact, it's my favorite scrapbooking method.

ⓘ TECH TIP

If you're low on computer memory or processing power, then **150–200 ppi** will do in a pinch. However, if you use elements from the *Digital Designs for Scrapbooking* CD, those elements will be at **300 ppi**, so you'll have to resize them to fit onto your page.

ⓘ TECH TIP

If you're worried about the archival quality of your printed pages, the definitive source for all things regarding archival printing is the Wilhelm Imaging Research web site, at wilhelm-research.com. There, you can check the archival ratings of your favorite printers, inks, and papers. You can also refer to your inkjet papers' packaging to see if they're archival.

Why mix the two? Often, it's to add texture to the physical page. Or, if you're like me, maybe you just like to play with all the scrapbooking tools and toys!

There are no "rules" when it comes to combining digital and traditional paper scrapbooking. Everything you already know about traditional scrapbooking still applies. Your favorite adhesives, embellishments and tools can work for you on a digitally created page, too.

One easy technique is to create the layouts in digital format, then print the photos on your favorite photo paper and attach them to the page. That gives the page a nice handmade feel. Or, leave areas in your layout empty and after you print your page, add purchased embellishments such as ribbons, charms or brads.

QUALITY BINDING

Some albums, such as wedding or gift albums, deserve special treatment. Good news! There are companies that will take your digital pages and bind them into beautiful, heirloom quality albums. ❺

Many of the online photo processing services that you use to print your photos also offer binding services. Shutterfly.com. ❻ snapfish.com, and even Walmart.com all offer binding. Sites, such as Bound2Remember.com and HeritageMakers.com, ❼ specialize in binding scrapbook albums and offer an even wider variety of styles and quality. If you're a Mac user, you can use the iPhoto software package from Apple to order a bound album. The styles are seemingly endless, so you're sure to find just what you're looking for.

USING CROP MARKS TO TRIM YOUR PAGES

There are two versions of all the 6 x 6 and 8 x 8 backgrounds, schemes and templates on the *Digital Designs for Scrapbooking* CD. If you're planning to print your pages, you'll want to use the versions with crop marks so you can trim the finished page to the

❺ *Printed and bound photo album "favorite family photos 2004" by Donna Downey.*

❻ *Shutterfly home page*

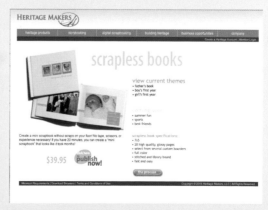

❼ *Heritagemakers.com*

correct size. ❶ If you're only going to view the pages online, use the version without crop marks.

Crop marks help you trim your pages accurately, with no white paper showing.

To trim a page, it's best to use a straight-edge cutting tool, such as a rotary trimmer, arm cutter, or craft knife and straight-edge. The crop marks are located at each corner of the page. If you line up your cutting edge with the crop marks, your cuts will be straight and accurate. Here's how:

crop marks ⟶

❶ Crop marks help you trim your pages accurately

STEP 1 Choose a scheme with crop marks, design and print out your page. ❷

STEP 2 Select one side of the page and align the crop marks with the edge of your cutter/trimmer. Trim that side of the page. ❸

STEP 3 Turn the page and align the next side's crop marks with the cutter. Trim that side and repeat once more. Three sides are now trimmed. ❹

STEP 5 Because you've trimmed away all of the crop marks, you need to measure for your last trim. Measure and align the page so that you trim away the excess and have exactly 8″ or 6″ remaining (depending on the page size you're using).

That's all there is to it. ❺

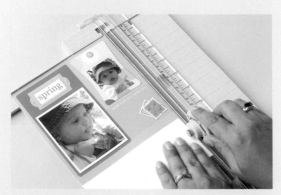

❷ Your printed page showing the crop marks.

❹ Trim three sides using the crop marks as a guide.

❸ Align crop marks with your cutter and trim first side.

❺ The perfectly trimmed page.

digital albums and displays

While it's fun to sit on the couch and look at a printed photo album with a special friend or two, the reality is that most of us have friends and family scattered all over the town, state, country or globe. For many digital scrapbookers, the easiest and most practical way to share their scrapbooks is online.

SLIDE SHOWS

Digital scrapbooking is exploding in popularity, and so are the options for sharing those digital albums. One of my favorites is to create a slide show.

To make a slide show of your pages, you'll need to choose a presentation software package. Two popular packages are Microsoft's PowerPoint (for Windows and Mac) and Apple's Keynote (Mac only). While these programs are designed for business presentations, they work just as well for creating digital albums.

To create a slide show of your digital pages, follow these steps:

STEP 1 After you've created your scrapbook pages using Adobe Photoshop Elements and the *Digital Designs for Scrapbooking* elements, save each layout page as a .jpg file. (When the **JPEG Options** dialog box appears, set the **Image Options** to Maximum, and leave the rest of the options at their default settings.)

STEP 2 Open your presentation software and set up your page size to match the size of your layouts.

STEP 3 Using the instructions that came with your software, insert your .jpg files, one page per slide and produce your slide show.

After you've saved your show, email it to family and friends or burn it to CD and send it as a gift.

In the gallery of albums in the next section, you can see an example of a slide show I made from the Greenwich Collection. The gallery's images are from my digital holiday greeting slide show, and include the CD, a case I decorated and pages from the slide show.

PRINTING A CD LABEL FROM THE CATALOG

With *Digital Designs for Scrapbooking*, not only are all your scrapbook pages beautifully coordinated, but now even your CDs can be coordinated!

In the Extras folder on the *Digital Designs for Scrapbooking* CD, you'll find CD label templates for each of the collections. ❶

These labels are designed to be printed on Fellowes Neato US CD Labels (2-up) paper. Printed labels are easily applied to your CD with their applicator. You can buy this label paper at an office supply store.

In each CD label template file, you'll find two round labels for the CD and two matching rectangular labels for the CD's case or spine. Treat the template as you would any page layout. Just add your information to the label (such as the title and date), then print the document. You can find more information about Fellowes Neato labels at neato.com.

USING A PAGE AS YOUR DESKTOP WALLPAPER

Are you particularly proud of a page and want to use it as wallpaper on your computer desktop? Or perhaps you'd like to use several pages as a screensaver. Check the help or documentation for your computer's operating system for instructions on how to set up wallpapers and screensavers.

Keep in mind that the page size you used for your page may not fit very well on your computer screen, so you may want to design a page format that will fit more closely to the aspect ratio of your screen.

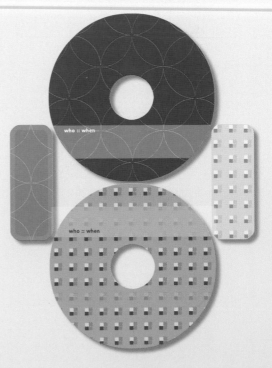

❶ *The sdcdlbl.png file is included on this book's accompanying cd.*

resource websites & books for more information

The community of digital scrapbookers is growing faster than you can imagine, and so is the amount of information and advice available to you on every possible topic related to digital scrapbooking.

There are so many online resources of interest to digital scrapbookers, I couldn't possibly cover them all in this book. (A much more comprehensive list appears in *Digital Scrapbooking 3*, available from Simple Scrapbooks.) But here are just a few of my favorite resources— places you can go to learn more about Adobe Photoshop Elements and about digital scrapbooking in general. (Remember, you can do a search for "digital scrapbooking" on the Internet to find thousands of other websites.)

Websites of Interest

adobe.com. ❶ Keep up with the latest news about Photoshop Elements. This site is frequently updated with user tips and techniques.

scrapbook-bytes.com. An online store and community devoted to digital scrapbooking.

digitalscrapbookplace.com. Another digital scrapbooking community.

groups.yahoo.com/group/computer-scrapping. A discussion group on digital scrapbooking.

twopeasinabucket.com. ❷ This popular scrapbooking site has an active digital discussion group.

Last, but not least, is my blog (weblog) at

❶ www.adobe.com

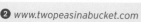

❷ www.twopeasinabucket.com

❸ www.reneepearson.typepad.com

reneepearson.typepad.com, ❸ a place you can always find me. From time to time I'll post tips and techniques and information of interest to digital scrapbookers.

Books on Adobe Photoshop Elements

Adobe Photoshop Elements 3.0 Classroom in a Book by Adobe Creative Team. ❹ The best tutorial-based book covering all the features of Photoshop Elements.

Photoshop Elements 3 One-on-One by Deke McClelland. A great all-purpose reference book.

Photoshop Elements 3 Down and Dirty Tricks by Scott Kelby. All the quick tips and tricks you need to get amazing results from Photoshop Elements. (It's also a fun read.)

Adobe Photoshop Elements One-Click Wow! by Jack Davis. ❺ This book comes with a CD that has over 600 instant effects, brushes, patterns, textures and gradients.

the beginning of a beautiful relationship...

Because Photoshop Elements is such a comprehensive program, there's no way we could cover all of its features in this book. So as you work with the software, be adventurous. Explore new features, try new options, and browse the Adobe Photoshop Elements **Help** for ideas. There are enough features in the software to keep you creating for a long, long time.

Enjoy!

❹ Adobe Photoshop Elements 3.0 Classroom in a Book.

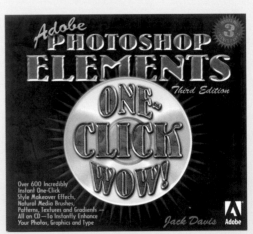

❺ Adobe Photoshop Elements 3.0 One-Click Wow! *contains a CD full of special effects.*

digital album gallery

As every scrapbooker knows, one of the greatest benefits of this hobby is the wonderful people you meet along the way. I've certainly met more than my share. There are three in particular whose skills I hold in high regard. And best of all, they're really nice people, too! I'm proud to call these ladies my friends, and prouder still of the beautiful albums they made using my designs.

In this chapter:

- Cathy Zielske and the Oak Park Collection
- Donna Downey and the Morningside Collection
- Molly Newman and the Sedona Collection
- Renee Pearson and the Greenwich Collection.

let me tell you a story

a collection of random stories from throughout my life

1966–2005

Cathy wrote and told me that she'd been wanting to do an album about her early life and thought the Oak Park Collection would be perfect.

Cathy Zielske

OAK PARK COLLECTION

My friend Cathy has redefined "simple scrapbooking" with her graphic design approach. Because her trademark style is timeless, her book, *Clean and Simple Scrapbooking*, is sure to be a perennial best seller. Since Cathy focuses on the story she's telling, her pages are not only attractive but compelling as well. I knew Cathy would give my Oak Park designs a unique showcase.

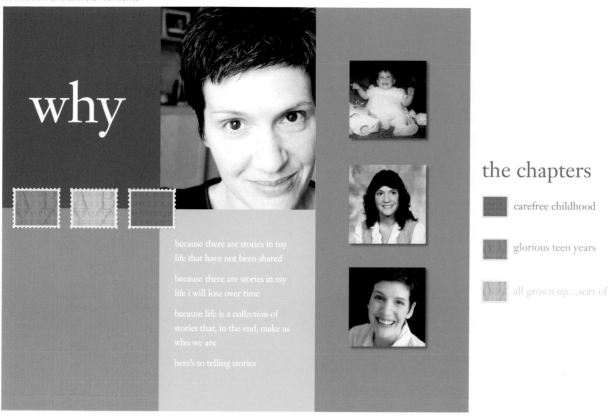

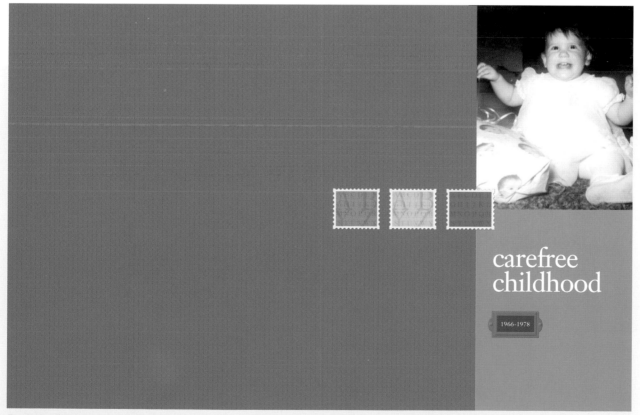

For Cathy, it's always about the story. For this album, it's about the random stories of her childhood and teen years. Cathy intends to make this an evolving album.

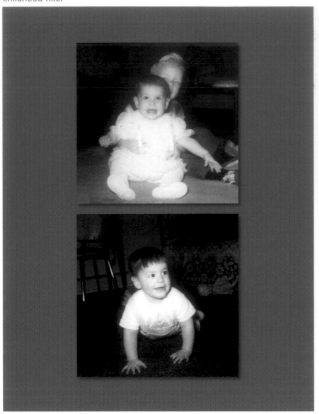

jc penney's special

One of the earliest stories I can recall sharing with people was that of being adopted. It was a short story, mind you. In the 1960s-closed-adoption climate, your adoptive parents were given little or no information about where their little bundle of joy came from. A little heritage, and a few seeimngly inconsequential details. That was it. And there you were.

I always loved to tell people, "I am adopted!" I think it always made me feel special. My parents were always very open about it. I never remember learning that I was adopted. It was just always "there."

I felt like it made me different, but in a good way. I'm not one of those people who has issues with being adopted, nor have I ever had the burning need to know more. I have two parents who love me more than anything in the world. They comforted me when I was sad, supported me when I was weak, and celebrated me when I succeeded—or failed—at anything. They changed my diapers, tied my shoes, packed my lunches, mediated fights between me and my brother, doled out discipline as needed, and never reserved love for a special occasion. Isn't that what makes a parent? Birthing a child a parent, makes not. I truly believe that. As awkward as the syntax sounds.

My mom used to tell me she ordered me from the JC Penney's catalog, and not once did she ever consider asking for a refund. It never failed to make me smile. I'm smiling right now as I remember.

And I still like telling people my short story of being adopted. Although, at 39, the story isn't really that short anymore, is it?

the lovely
teen years

1979-1984

Using a consistent and simple grid scheme, Cathy created her pages using Adobe Photoshop CS and InDesign CS.

Let Me Tell You a Story is an evolving album, a personal journal of Cathy's history.

FIGURE ROLLER SKATING

the next dorothy hamill?

Make that the next Natalie Dunn, to be more precise. Oh, you've never heard of Natalie Dunn, who, in the late '70s and early '80s was on the same par as Dorothy Hamill? Well, of course you haven't. She was a figure roller skater. And, the thriving sport of figure roller skating got absolutely no coverage on television. How do I know this? Simple: I was a teen-aged figure roller skater.

While technically I started when I was 11, skating dominated my formative teen years. Five days a week, two to four hours a day. Practicing, falling, running through routines, falling, and most importantly, socializing. Skating was my life. (And my mother's as well.) I still can't believe, now that I'm grown, with children, just how much time my mother gave of herself, to see that her daughter could pursue her athletic dream.

I was never that good. But in retrospect, it didn't matter. I had a modicum of natural ability, but only on the presentation level. I put together my own music, and choreographed my own routines. I just never quite nailed the jumping aspect of it all. I remember going through minor depressions when I realized, fairly early on, that I was never going to be "the bomb." (Although we didn't use the term "the bomb" in the early '80s. But I think what it did for me, is allow me to build confidence in myself. It allowed me to be physical and graceful at the same time. It taught me how to lose and win gracefully, and the value of dedication.

It also provided a fun, safe and healthy alternative to getting into any teen-aged trouble. Though I still managed to find ways to do that. It gave me a supportive framework in which to grow up. I think being a skater helped me to become the person I am today.

Just don't ask me to try on the old costumes.

materials
OAK PARK COLLECTION
8½ x 11 Album – Archivers
Ribbon – Offray
Font – Janson by Adobe

When Donna saw the Morningside Collection she pointed and said "mine." Donna was immediately attracted to the strong patterns and contemporary colors which helped to convey her feelings for her "boys" -- hubby Bill and son Cole.

One of the first words Cole ever spoke was "da-da", which now at 18 months has evolved "da-di" with the occasional "be-ill" throw just for good measure as a reminder to u is now able to repeat almost anything he Bill was so excited when the nurse turned to the doctor's office and said, "It's a boy." Maybe even a bit shocked. He had prepared himself to hear we were going to be having another girl, but had not even considered his reaction upon hearing it was a boy. It wasn't until hours later that the news had finally begun to sink in and it wasn't long before Bill had shared the news with anyone that would listen. Cole has made our family complete.

Donna Downey

MORNINGSIDE COLLECTION

Donna is the queen of creative scrapbooking. I'm convinced she can make a scrapbook out of anything. In fact, her *"Yes It's a Scrapbook"* series of books are about just that. Her delightful paper bag album demonstrates how well the Morningside Collection's digital backgrounds work with "real" techniques and embellishments.

Donna decided to make a paper bag album, "Because it was trendy and I wanted to try and make one." The natural pockets served as perfect containers to hide her journaling tags.

To make the basic album, Donna layered three lunch bags in opposite directions then folded them in half to create a spine. She punched holes in the spine and bound the album with elastic.

Even though Bill refers to Cole as his "litt[...]n" he is definitely his mother's son, and if I [...] be totally honest...I LOVE every minute[...] Cole is pure laughter, silliness and a wea[...] affection. As he begins to learn more and mo[...] about his surroundings he grows even more irresistible. He is both rough and tumble and lovable all packaged in one adorable exterior...so adorable that I can't help but squeeze him every chance I get. But my favorite moment of the day is when I lay him down in his crib at night and say "night, night Coley" and he repeats back "nite, nite...iwufu."...priceless!

Donna kept her embellishments simple and within the color scheme. She created her journaling tags on her computer then trimmed and painted the edges. Finally, Donna added stickers, ribbons and paint to give her album that unique "Donna" touch.

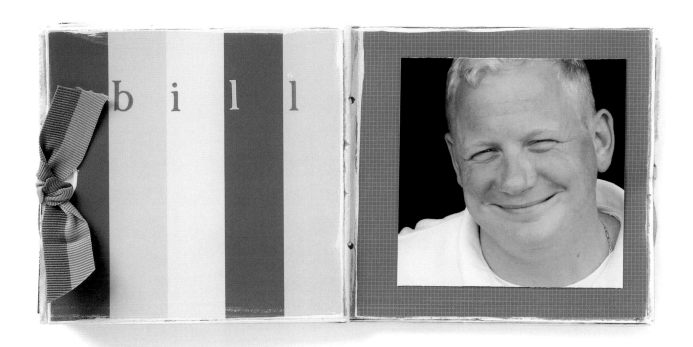

My sexy man! My hubby is such a hotty, and has only gotten more attractive as he has gotten older....older being all relative since he is 3 years younger than me. From the moment he asked me out, I knew that he was THE ONE...sensitive, loving and strong. He loves me like no other person has ever loved me before and I feel safe just knowing he is taking care of me and our family. Marriage and a family has worn a lot on our relationship but as life changes, with its ups and downs, I know that the one constant in my life is Bill and his love for me. He loves unconditionally and without judgment. He is the love of my life.

materials
MORNINGSIDE COLLECTION
Font - Times New Roman
Letter stickers - Chatterbox
Chipboard frame - L'il Davis
Ribbon - L'il Davis
Elastic - 7gypsies
Acrylic paint
Stamping ink

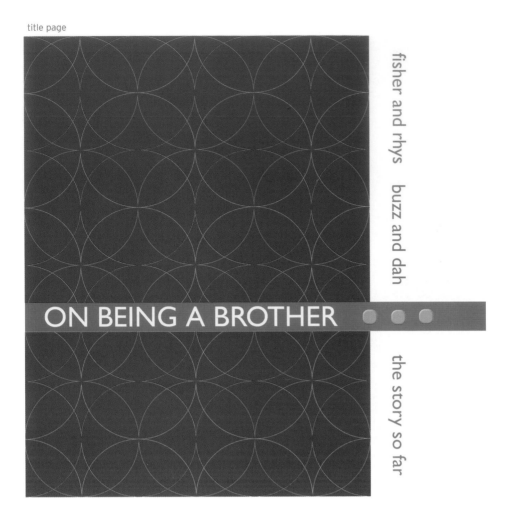

ON BEING A BROTHER

fisher and rhys   buzz and dah

the story so far

Molly Newman

SEDONA COLLECTION

Molly's skills are admired throughout the digital scrapbooking community. Her work as editor of the *Simple Scrapbooks* digital special issues has helped so many scrapbookers hone their digital skills. When designing the finishing touches to the Sedona Collection, I had Molly with her stunning red hair and witty personality in mind.

contents

growing up

learn & play

xoxoxo

don't forget

growing up section opener

fisher 5.3.99

rhys 4.20.01

growing up

4 years & counting

With its bright colors and geometrics, Molly thought the Sedona Collection was perfect for a fun, playful album about her sons—an album she'd wanted to do for a long time.

growing up filler

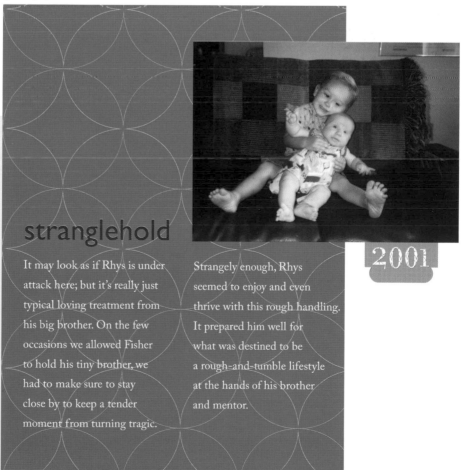

Molly created the entire album in Adobe Photoshop Elements 3 using just the elements in the kit. By leaving the design simple and straightforward, she left lots of room for journaling about her favorite subject— her kids.

stranglehold

It may look as if Rhys is under attack here; but it's really just typical loving treatment from his big brother. On the few occasions we allowed Fisher to hold his tiny brother, we had to make sure to stay close by to keep a tender moment from turning tragic.

Strangely enough, Rhys seemed to enjoy and even thrive with this rough handling. It prepared him well for what was destined to be a rough-and-tumble lifestyle at the hands of his brother and mentor.

2001

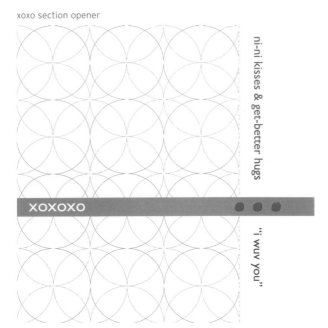

ni-ni kisses & get-better hugs

XOXOXO

"i wuv you"

Molly used a simple technique to create the overlay of white journaling on her photo (below). She duplicated the text layer, changed the text color to white, chose "Simplify Layer" then deleted all the areas of the layer that didn't overlap the photo.

huggybugs

Both these boys are natural-born snugglers. From the footsteps padding down the hallway for a morning snug with Mama and Papa to Fisher's arm thrown over a sleeping Rhys at night, there is nothing they respond to like love and affection.

They give each other hugs and snuggles all day long. Fisher cheers up Rhys with lavish kisses and Rhys favors Fisher with multiple "I wuv yous" every day. We hope they always have such powerful feelings of attachment for each other (and their parents too).

2004

materials
SEDONA COLLECTION
8 x 8 Album - Colorbök
Fonts - Gill Sans MT (titles),
Adobe Caslon Pro (journaling)
Letter Sticker - American Crafts

learn and play section opener

legos & star wars & knights

learn and play ● ● ●

abcs & 123s

learn and play filler

2005

MIRROR

reflection

If imitation is the sincerest form of flattery, Fisher ought to feel very flattered by Rhys' constant imitation of everything he does. Whether it's a slang term ("Duuuuuude, cooooooool!") or a leisure-time obsession, Rhys is the eternal student & sidekick.

Rhys is Robin to Fisher's Batman, Daredevil to his Spider-Man, Darth Vader to his Anakin Skywalker (we're still not sure how that one is physically possible), Rocky Canyon to his Billy Blazes. This seems to suit them both just fine...

To print her album pages, Molly uploaded the files to a photo developing Web site and had each printed as an 8 x 10 photo. Then she trimmed 1" from the top and bottom of each print and inserted them in a standard post-bound album.

title page

The title and dedication pages set the tone for the rest of the album. Since I wouldn't be printing these pages I could make them any shape I wanted. To carry-through on the CD concept I chose the circle. Lowering the opacity of the photo allowed my journaling to stand out.

Renee Pearson

GREENWICH COLLECTION

While designing this collection, I always envisioned it used to make an elegant Christmas album. Now that my husband Kent and I are empty nesters, I thought it would be fun to send out digital holiday greetings with highlights of our year of "freedom". So, I've used the Greenwich collection to create a PowerPoint slide show I'll burn to CD and send to family and close friends this holiday season.

To decorate the packaging I printed two Greenwich CD labels, applied one to the CD and the other to the case. I'd been saving this huge flower, detached from a gift bag, waiting for the perfect opportunity to use it.

love

what goes around

ultimately comes around
and our state of empty nestdom
brings with it new freedom
in other words…

we're having a ball!

Seal concert :: June '05

dedication page

New York Book Expo :: June '05

renee

dreams do come true

a new career as
a published author

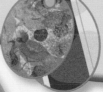

filler pages

kent

putting in the miles
everyday
paid off at the Peachtree

Peachtree Road Race :: July '05

*This is where the circular format I chose became
tricky. The trick? Create a square layout first, then use
the shape and masking techniques you've learned to
adjust the photo positions and crop into a circle shape.*

While not perfectly posed, this photo is so my family! Always moving, always busy. And it's our first family photo with my grandson, Sebastian, included. The simple lyrics to a familiar holiday song capped it all.

matt   renee   johanna
tamara   chris   kent
and **sebastian**

our brood today

New York Book Expo :: June '05

kent

meeting spencer tillman
bonding with tamara

we wish you a merry christmas

we wish you a merry christmas

we wish you a merry christmas

and a happy new year

happy
holidays

materials
GREENWICH COLLECTION

CD case - Boxer Scrapbooks
Fonts - Dalliance by Emigre (word art titles), Avenir by Linotype (journaling)

cd catalog

Eager to check out the goodies on the CD? I don't blame you. I've read

your comments on the scrapbooking message boards and knew you'd

love to have a visual catalog of all the digital backgrounds and elements,

someplace you could go to plan your pages before getting started. That's

how I hope you'll use this section.

Everything on the *Digital Designs for Scrapbooking* CD is organized into folders, starting with the four coordinated collections: **Greenwich, Morningside, Oak Park** and **Sedona.** The six backgrounds and one overlay in each collection come in four sizes: 6 x 6", 8 x 8", 8.5 x 11" and 12 x 12". The first three come with and without crop marks or borders. You can identify those without crop marks by the "edg" attached to their file names. They can be used if you have a printer that will print to the edge of a page or if you don't intend to print your pages. The collections folders also contain the photo-ready page templates.

While the elements are grouped with their design collections, feel free to mix and match them. I've designed many of them to be interchangeable between collections. The elements have very small shadows, so you can add additional shadow effects if you choose.

The digital Simple Schemes are layered files collected in their own folder. Everything else (crop mark templates, CD label templates and color swatch palettes) is in the **Extras** folder. Remember, you can also use the **File Browser** in Adobe Photoshop Elements to view thumbnails of everything.

greenwich

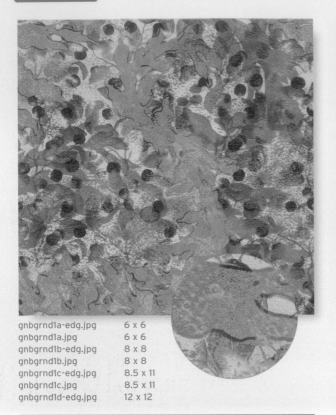

gnbgrnd1a-edg.jpg	6 x 6
gnbgrnd1a.jpg	6 x 6
gnbgrnd1b-edg.jpg	8 x 8
gnbgrnd1b.jpg	8 x 8
gnbgrnd1c-edg.jpg	8.5 x 11
gnbgrnd1c.jpg	8.5 x 11
gnbgrnd1d-edg.jpg	12 x 12

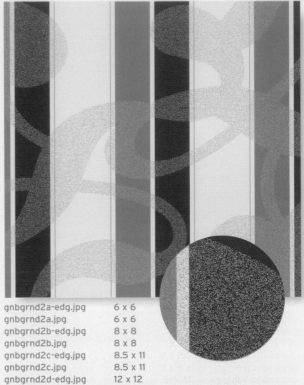

gnbgrnd2a-edg.jpg	6 x 6
gnbgrnd2a.jpg	6 x 6
gnbgrnd2b-edg.jpg	8 x 8
gnbgrnd2b.jpg	8 x 8
gnbgrnd2c-edg.jpg	8.5 x 11
gnbgrnd2c.jpg	8.5 x 11
gnbgrnd2d-edg.jpg	12 x 12

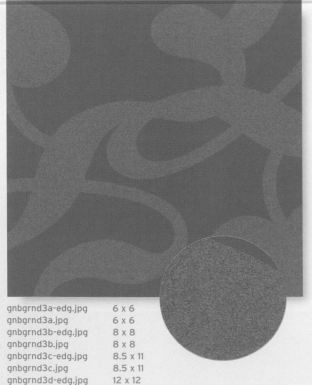

gnbgrnd3a-edg.jpg	6 x 6
gnbgrnd3a.jpg	6 x 6
gnbgrnd3b-edg.jpg	8 x 8
gnbgrnd3b.jpg	8 x 8
gnbgrnd3c-edg.jpg	8.5 x 11
gnbgrnd3c.jpg	8.5 x 11
gnbgrnd3d-edg.jpg	12 x 12

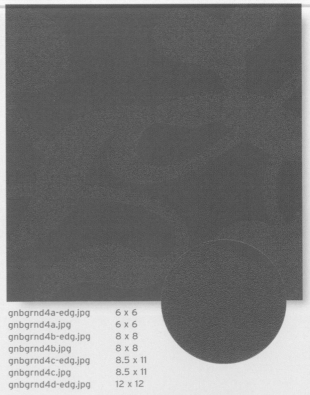

gnbgrnd4a-edg.jpg	6 x 6
gnbgrnd4a.jpg	6 x 6
gnbgrnd4b-edg.jpg	8 x 8
gnbgrnd4b.jpg	8 x 8
gnbgrnd4c-edg.jpg	8.5 x 11
gnbgrnd4c.jpg	8.5 x 11
gnbgrnd4d-edg.jpg	12 x 12

gnbgrnd5a-edg.jpg   6 x 6
gnbgrnd5a.jpg   6 x 6
gnbgrnd5b-edg.jpg   8 x 8
gnbgrnd5b.jpg   8 x 8
gnbgrnd5c-edg.jpg   8.5 x 11
gnbgrnd5c.jpg   8.5 x 11
gnbgrnd5d-edg.jpg   12 x 12

gnbgrnd6a-edg.jpg   6 x 6
gnbgrnd6a.jpg   6 x 6
gnbgrnd6b-edg.jpg   8 x 8
gnbgrnd6b.jpg   8 x 8
gnbgrnd6c-edg.jpg   8.5 x 11
gnbgrnd6c.jpg   8.5 x 11
gnbgrnd6d-edg.jpg   12 x 12

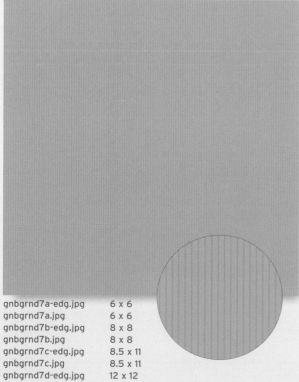

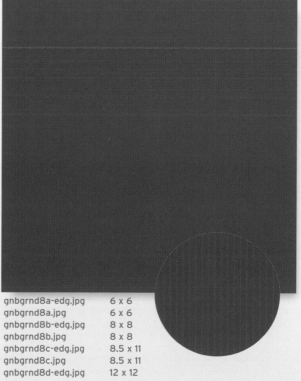

gnbgrnd7a-edg.jpg   6 x 6
gnbgrnd7a.jpg   6 x 6
gnbgrnd7b-edg.jpg   8 x 8
gnbgrnd7b.jpg   8 x 8
gnbgrnd7c-edg.jpg   8.5 x 11
gnbgrnd7c.jpg   8.5 x 11
gnbgrnd7d-edg.jpg   12 x 12

gnbgrnd8a-edg.jpg   6 x 6
gnbgrnd8a.jpg   6 x 6
gnbgrnd8b-edg.jpg   8 x 8
gnbgrnd8b.jpg   8 x 8
gnbgrnd8c-edg.jpg   8.5 x 11
gnbgrnd8c.jpg   8.5 x 11
gnbgrnd8d-edg.jpg   12 x 12

greenwich

gralphasheet.png

grbkplts.png

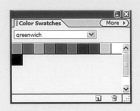

greenwich.aco
color swatch for Greenwich Collection
(file is in "color_swatches" in "Extras" folder)

grbrads.png

grbuttons.png

grconchos.png

grcorners.png

grlabels.png

grstamps.png

grtags.png

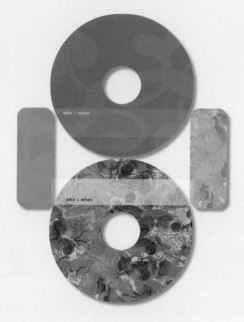

grovrly1a.png   6 x 6
grovrly1b.png   8 x 8
grovrly1c.png   8.5 x 11
grovrly1d.png   12 x 12

grcdlbl.png
cd label for Greenwich Collection
(file is in "Extras" folder)

TEMPLATES

grtmplttl.jpg
grtmplttl-edg.jpg

grtmplded.jpg
grtmplded-edg.jpg

greenwich

grtmpltoc.jpg
grtmpltoc-edg.jpg

grtmplsec.jpg
grtmplsec-edg.jpg

grtmplfil1.jpg
grtmplfil1-edg.jpg

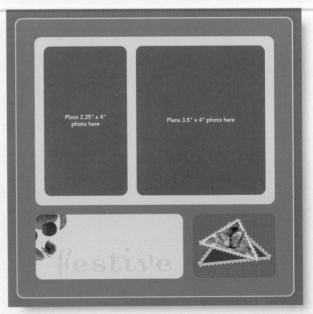

grtmplfil2.jpg
grtmplfil2-edg.jpg

morningside

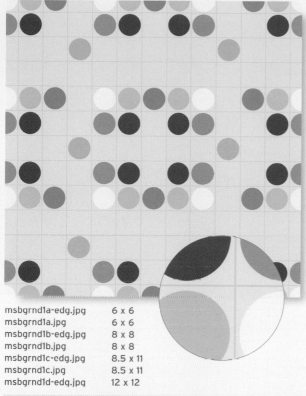

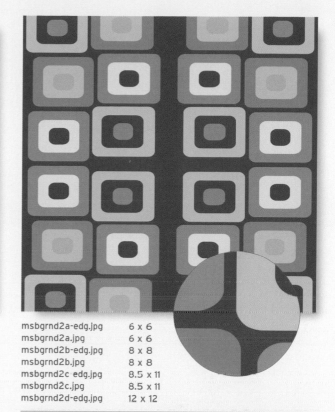

msbgrnd1a-edg.jpg	6 x 6
msbgrnd1a.jpg	6 x 6
msbgrnd1b-edg.jpg	8 x 8
msbgrnd1b.jpg	8 x 8
msbgrnd1c-edg.jpg	8.5 x 11
msbgrnd1c.jpg	8.5 x 11
msbgrnd1d-edg.jpg	12 x 12

msbgrnd2a-edg.jpg	6 x 6
msbgrnd2a.jpg	6 x 6
msbgrnd2b-edg.jpg	8 x 8
msbgrnd2b.jpg	8 x 8
msbgrnd2c-edg.jpg	8.5 x 11
msbgrnd2c.jpg	8.5 x 11
msbgrnd2d-edg.jpg	12 x 12

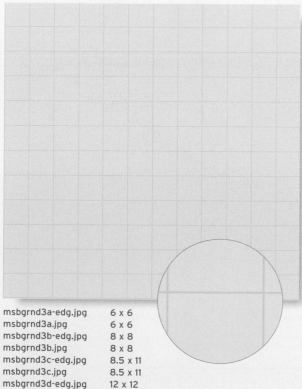

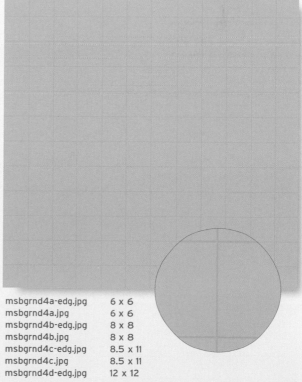

msbgrnd3a-edg.jpg	6 x 6
msbgrnd3a.jpg	6 x 6
msbgrnd3b-edg.jpg	8 x 8
msbgrnd3b.jpg	8 x 8
msbgrnd3c-edg.jpg	8.5 x 11
msbgrnd3c.jpg	8.5 x 11
msbgrnd3d-edg.jpg	12 x 12

msbgrnd4a-edg.jpg	6 x 6
msbgrnd4a.jpg	6 x 6
msbgrnd4b-edg.jpg	8 x 8
msbgrnd4b.jpg	8 x 8
msbgrnd4c-edg.jpg	8.5 x 11
msbgrnd4c.jpg	8.5 x 11
msbgrnd4d-edg.jpg	12 x 12

morningside

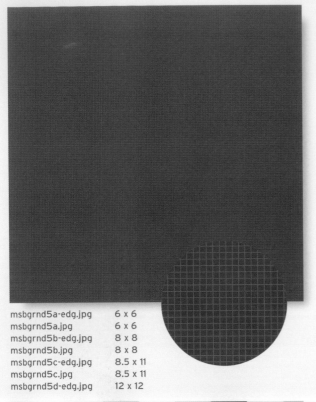

msbgrnd5a-edg.jpg	6 x 6
msbgrnd5a.jpg	6 x 6
msbgrnd5b-edg.jpg	8 x 8
msbgrnd5b.jpg	8 x 8
msbgrnd5c-edg.jpg	8.5 x 11
msbgrnd5c.jpg	8.5 x 11
msbgrnd5d-edg.jpg	12 x 12

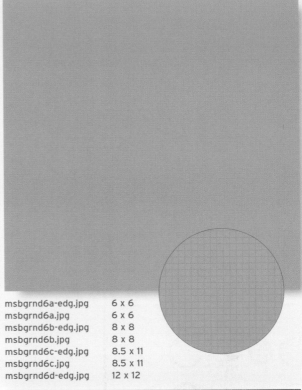

msbgrnd6a-edg.jpg	6 x 6
msbgrnd6a.jpg	6 x 6
msbgrnd6b-edg.jpg	8 x 8
msbgrnd6b.jpg	8 x 8
msbgrnd6c-edg.jpg	8.5 x 11
msbgrnd6c.jpg	8.5 x 11
msbgrnd6d-edg.jpg	12 x 12

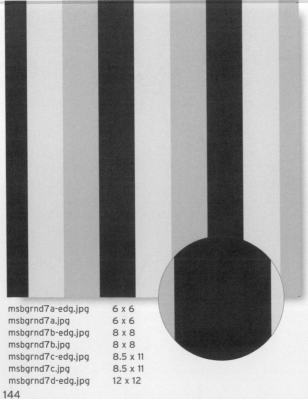

msbgrnd7a-edg.jpg	6 x 6
msbgrnd7a.jpg	6 x 6
msbgrnd7b-edg.jpg	8 x 8
msbgrnd7b.jpg	8 x 8
msbgrnd7c-edg.jpg	8.5 x 11
msbgrnd7c.jpg	8.5 x 11
msbgrnd7d-edg.jpg	12 x 12

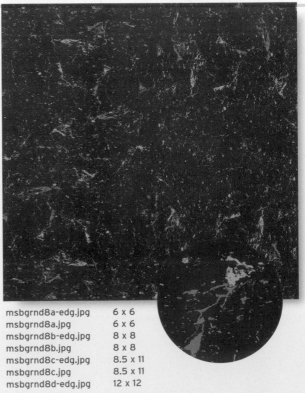

msbgrnd8a-edg.jpg	6 x 6
msbgrnd8a.jpg	6 x 6
msbgrnd8b-edg.jpg	8 x 8
msbgrnd8b.jpg	8 x 8
msbgrnd8c-edg.jpg	8.5 x 11
msbgrnd8c.jpg	8.5 x 11
msbgrnd8d-edg.jpg	12 x 12

msalphasheet.png

msbkplts.png

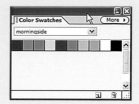

morningside.aco
color swatch for Morningside Collection
(file is in "color_swatches" in "Extras" folder)

msbrads.png

msbuttons.png

msconchos.png

I finally figured the only reason to be alive is to enjoy it
rita may brown

msovrly2.png

mstabs.png

msstamps.png

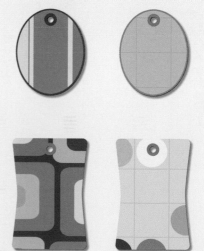

mstags.png

145

morningside

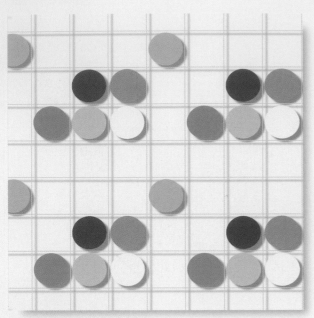

msovrly1a.png 6 x 6
msovrly1b.png 8 x 8
msovrly1c.png 8.5 x 11
msovrly1d.png 12 x 12

mscdlbl.png
cd label for Morningside Collection
(file is in "Extras" folder)

Place 4.5" x 3.4" photo here

mstmplttl.jpg
mstmplttl-edg.jpg

mstmplded.jpg
mstmplded-edg.jpg

mstmpltoc.jpg
mstmpltoc-edg.jpg

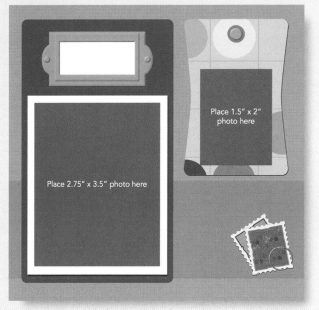

mstmplsec.jpg
mstmplsec-edg.jpg

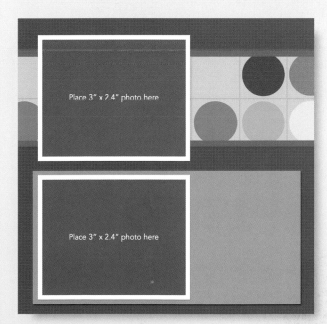

mstmpfll1.jpg
mstmpfll1-edg.jpg

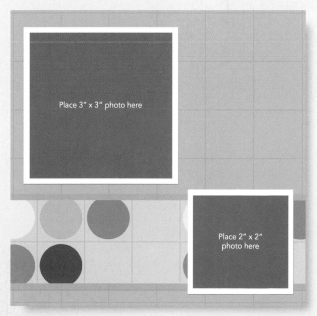

mstmplfil2.jpg
mstmplfil2-edg.jpg

oak park

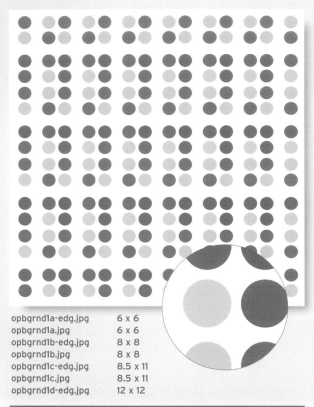

opbgrnd1a-edg.jpg	6 x 6
opbgrnd1a.jpg	6 x 6
opbgrnd1b-edg.jpg	8 x 8
opbgrnd1b.jpg	8 x 8
opbgrnd1c-edg.jpg	8.5 x 11
opbgrnd1c.jpg	8.5 x 11
opbgrnd1d-edg.jpg	12 x 12

opbgrnd2a-edg.jpg	6 x 6
opbgrnd2a.jpg	6 x 6
opbgrnd2b-edg.jpg	8 x 8
opbgrnd2b.jpg	8 x 8
opbgrnd2c-edg.jpg	8.5 x 11
opbgrnd2c.jpg	8.5 x 11
opbgrnd2d-edg.jpg	12 x 12

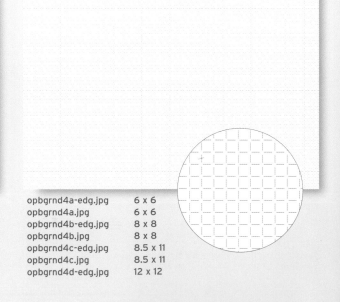

opbgrnd3a-edg.jpg	6 x 6
opbgrnd3a.jpg	6 x 6
opbgrnd3b-edg.jpg	8 x 8
opbgrnd3b.jpg	8 x 8
opbgrnd3c-edg.jpg	8.5 x 11
opbgrnd3c.jpg	8.5 x 11
opbgrnd3d-edg.jpg	12 x 12

opbgrnd4a-edg.jpg	6 x 6
opbgrnd4a.jpg	6 x 6
opbgrnd4b-edg.jpg	8 x 8
opbgrnd4b.jpg	8 x 8
opbgrnd4c-edg.jpg	8.5 x 11
opbgrnd4c.jpg	8.5 x 11
opbgrnd4d-edg.jpg	12 x 12

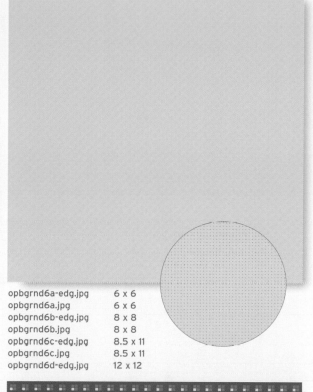

opbgrnd5a-edg.jpg	6 x 6
opbgrnd5a.jpg	6 x 6
opbgrnd5b-edg.jpg	8 x 8
opbgrnd5b.jpg	8 x 8
opbgrnd5c-edg.jpg	8.5 x 11
opbgrnd5c.jpg	8.5 x 11
opbgrnd5d-edg.jpg	12 x 12

opbgrnd6a-edg.jpg	6 x 6
opbgrnd6a.jpg	6 x 6
opbgrnd6b-edg.jpg	8 x 8
opbgrnd6b.jpg	8 x 8
opbgrnd6c-edg.jpg	8.5 x 11
opbgrnd6c.jpg	8.5 x 11
opbgrnd6d-edg.jpg	12 x 12

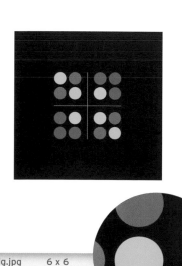

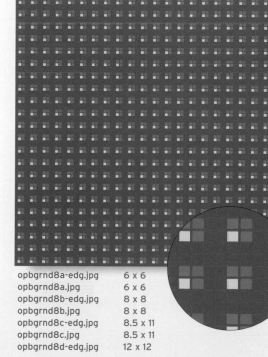

opbgrnd7a-edg.jpg	6 x 6
opbgrnd7a.jpg	6 x 6
opbgrnd7b-edg.jpg	8 x 8
opbgrnd7b.jpg	8 x 8
opbgrnd7c-edg.jpg	8.5 x 11
opbgrnd7c.jpg	8.5 x 11
opbgrnd7d-edg.jpg	12 x 12

opbgrnd8a-edg.jpg	6 x 6
opbgrnd8a.jpg	6 x 6
opbgrnd8b-edg.jpg	8 x 8
opbgrnd8b.jpg	8 x 8
opbgrnd8c-edg.jpg	8.5 x 11
opbgrnd8c.jpg	8.5 x 11
opbgrnd8d-edg.jpg	12 x 12

oak park

a b c d e f
g h i j k l
m n o p q r
s t u v w x
y z " , . ! ?
1 2 3 4 5
6 7 8 9 0

opalphasheet.png

opbkplts.png

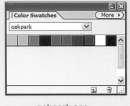

oakpark.aco
color swatch for Oakpark Collection
(file is in "color_swatches" in "Extras" folder)

opbrads.png

opbuttons.png

opconchos.png

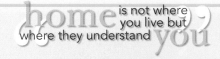

opovly6.png

is not where
you live but
where they understand

optabs.png

opstamps.png

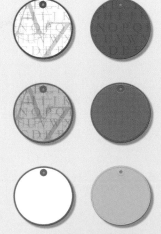

optags.png

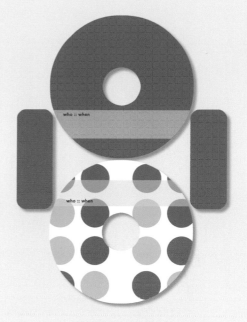

opovly1a.png
opovly1b.png
opovly1c.png
opovly1d.png

opcdlbl.png
cd label for Oak Park Collection
(file is in "Extras" folder)

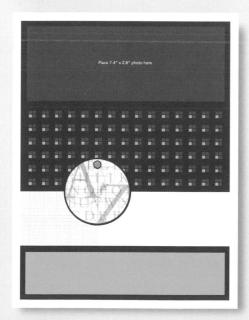

optmplttl.jpg

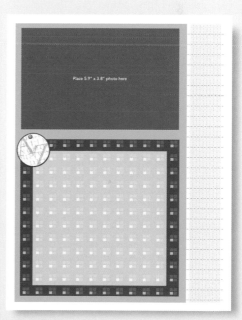

optplded.jpg

oak park

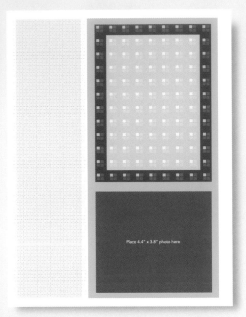

optmpltoc.jpg

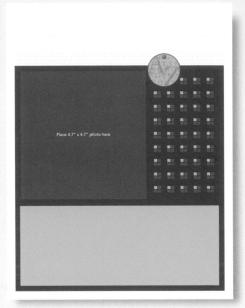

optmplsec.jpg

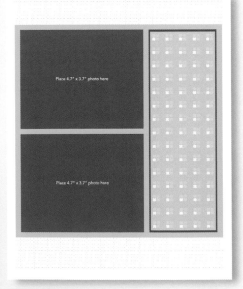

optmplfil1.jpg

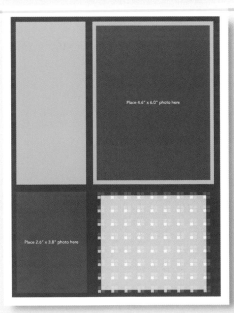

optmplfil2.jpg

sedona

BACKGROUNDS

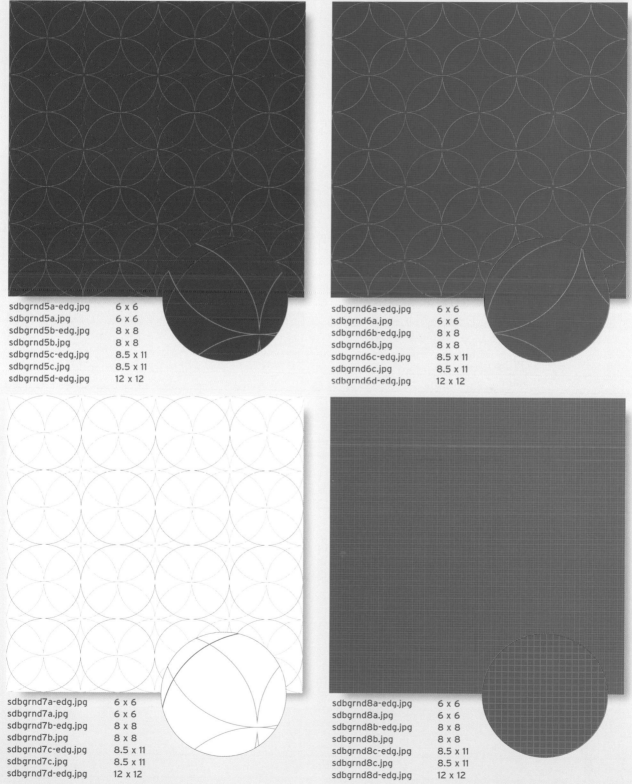

sdbgrnd5a-edg.jpg	6 x 6
sdbgrnd5a.jpg	6 x 6
sdbgrnd5b-edg.jpg	8 x 8
sdbgrnd5b.jpg	8 x 8
sdbgrnd5c-edg.jpg	8.5 x 11
sdbgrnd5c.jpg	8.5 x 11
sdbgrnd5d-edg.jpg	12 x 12

sdbgrnd6a-edg.jpg	6 x 6
sdbgrnd6a.jpg	6 x 6
sdbgrnd6b-edg.jpg	8 x 8
sdbgrnd6b.jpg	8 x 8
sdbgrnd6c-edg.jpg	8.5 x 11
sdbgrnd6c.jpg	8.5 x 11
sdbgrnd6d-edg.jpg	12 x 12

sdbgrnd7a-edg.jpg	6 x 6
sdbgrnd7a.jpg	6 x 6
sdbgrnd7b-edg.jpg	8 x 8
sdbgrnd7b.jpg	8 x 8
sdbgrnd7c-edg.jpg	8.5 x 11
sdbgrnd7c.jpg	8.5 x 11
sdbgrnd7d-edg.jpg	12 x 12

sdbgrnd8a-edg.jpg	6 x 6
sdbgrnd8a.jpg	6 x 6
sdbgrnd8b-edg.jpg	8 x 8
sdbgrnd8b.jpg	8 x 8
sdbgrnd8c-edg.jpg	8.5 x 11
sdbgrnd8c.jpg	8.5 x 11
sdbgrnd8d-edg.jpg	12 x 12

sedona

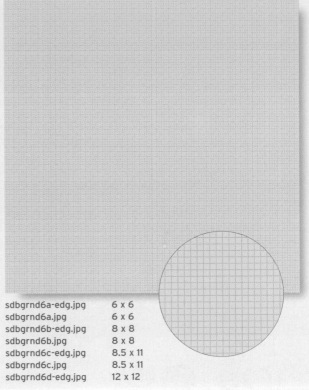

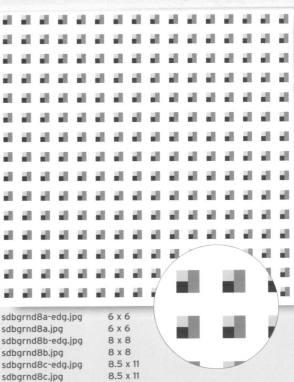

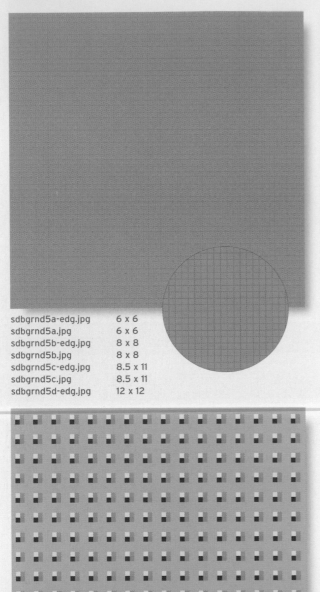

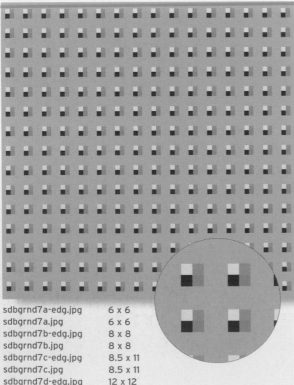

sdbgrnd5a-edg.jpg	6 x 6
sdbgrnd5a.jpg	6 x 6
sdbgrnd5b-edg.jpg	8 x 8
sdbgrnd5b.jpg	8 x 8
sdbgrnd5c-edg.jpg	8.5 x 11
sdbgrnd5c.jpg	8.5 x 11
sdbgrnd5d-edg.jpg	12 x 12

sdbgrnd6a-edg.jpg	6 x 6
sdbgrnd6a.jpg	6 x 6
sdbgrnd6b-edg.jpg	8 x 8
sdbgrnd6b.jpg	8 x 8
sdbgrnd6c-edg.jpg	8.5 x 11
sdbgrnd6c.jpg	8.5 x 11
sdbgrnd6d-edg.jpg	12 x 12

sdbgrnd7a-edg.jpg	6 x 6
sdbgrnd7a.jpg	6 x 6
sdbgrnd7b-edg.jpg	8 x 8
sdbgrnd7b.jpg	8 x 8
sdbgrnd7c-edg.jpg	8.5 x 11
sdbgrnd7c.jpg	8.5 x 11
sdbgrnd7d-edg.jpg	12 x 12

sdbgrnd8a-edg.jpg	6 x 6
sdbgrnd8a.jpg	6 x 6
sdbgrnd8b-edg.jpg	8 x 8
sdbgrnd8b.jpg	8 x 8
sdbgrnd8c-edg.jpg	8.5 x 11
sdbgrnd8c.jpg	8.5 x 11
sdbgrnd8d-edg.jpg	12 x 12

sdalphasheet.png

sdbkplts.png

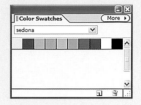

sedona.aco
color swatch for Sedona Collection
(file is in "color_swatches" in "Extras" folder)

sdbrads.png

sdbuttons.png

sdconchos.png

sdovly2.png

sdtabs.png

sdstamps.png

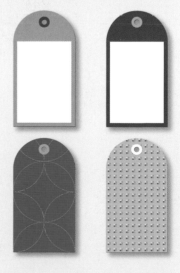

sdtags.png

sedona

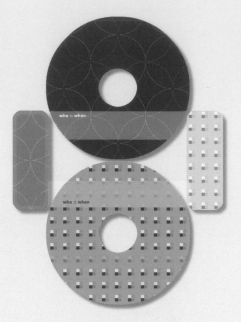

sdovrly1a.png	6 x 6
sdovrly1b.png	8 x 8
sdovrly1c.png	8.5 x 11
sdovrly1d.png	12 x 12

sdcdlbl.png
cd label for Sedona Collection
(file is in "Extras" folder)

sdtmplttl.jpg
sdtmplttl-edg.jpg

sdtmplded.jpg
sdtmplded-edg.jpg

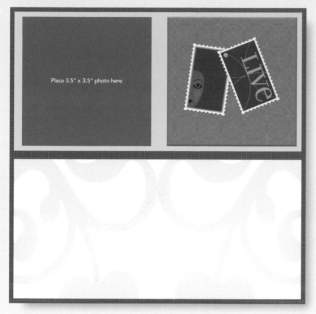

sdtmpltoc.jpg
sdtmpltoc-edg.jpg

sdtmplsec.jpg
sdtmplsec-edg.jpg

sdtmplfll1.jpg
sdtmplfll1-edg.jpg

sdtmplfll2.jpg
sdtmplfll2-edg.jpg

schemes

The next catalog images are thumbnails of the layered Simple Schemes on your CD. Simple Schemes are layout blueprints or page patterns. Replace each layer in the Simple Scheme with an item from my collections and your photographs, and see how fast and easy digital scrapbooking can be.

6schmttl-edg.psd   6 x 6
6schmttl.psd   6 x 6

6schmded-edg.psd   6 x 6
6schmded.psd   6 x 6

6schmtoc-edg.psd   6 x 6
6schmtoc.psd   6 x 6

6schmsec-edg.psd   6 x 6
6schmsec.psd   6 x 6

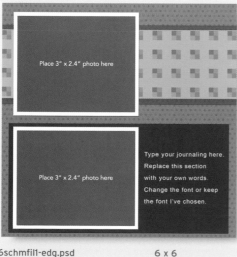

6schmfil1-edg.psd   6 x 6
6schmfil1.psd   6 x 6

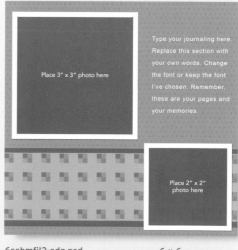

6schmfil2-edg.psd   6 x 6
6schmfil2.psd   6 x 6

Place 3.5" x 3.5" photo here

title.here

Type your journaling here.
Replace this section with your
title.here
own words. Change the font or keep
the font I've chosen. Remember, these
are your pages and your memories.
The schemes are blueprints designed
to make digital scrapbooking
quick and easy.

Place 3.75" x 3.75" photo here

Place 3.5" x 3.5" photo here

title.here

Type your journaling here. Replace this section with your own
words. Change the font or keep the font I've chosen.
Remember, these are your pages and your memories. The
schemes are blueprints designed to make digital scrapbooking
quick and easy.

8schmttl-edg.psd   8 x 8
8schmttl.psd   8 x 8

8schmded-edg.psd   8 x 8
8schmded.psd   8 x 8

title.here

.table entry 1

.table entry 2

.table entry 3

.table entry 4

.table entry 5

Place 3.5" x 3.5" photo here

Type your journaling here. Replace this section with your own
words. Change the font or keep the font I've chosen.
Remember, these are your pages and your memories. The
schemes are blueprints designed to make digital scrapbooking
quick and easy.

title.here

Place 3.5" x 3.5" photo here

8schmtoc-edg.psd   8 x 8
8schmtoc.psd   8 x 8

8schmsec-edg.psd   8 x 8
8schmsec.psd   8 x 8

Place 7.5" x 3.5" photo here

Place 3.75" x 3.75" photo here

Type your journaling here.
Replace this section with your
title.here
own words. Change the font or keep
the font I've chosen. Remember, these
are your pages and your memories.
The schemes are blueprints designed
to make digital scrapbooking
quick and easy.

Type your journaling here. Replace
this section with your own words.
Change the font or keep the font
I've chosen. Remember, these are
your pages and your memories.
The schemes are blueprints
title.here
designed to make digital scrapbooking quick and easy.

Place 3.75" x 3.75" photo here

Place 3.5" x 3.5" photo here

Place 3.5" x 3.5" photo here

8schmfil1-edg.psd   8 x 8
8schmfil1.psd   8 x 8

8schmfil2-edg.psd   8 x 8
8schmfil2.psd   8 x 8

82schmttl-edg.psd   8 x 8
82schmttl.psd   8 x 8

82schmded-edg.psd   8 x 8
82schmded.psd   8 x 8

82schmsec-edg.psd   8 x 8
82schmsec2.psd   8 x 8

82schmtoc-edg.psd   8 x 8
82schmtoc.psd   8 x 8

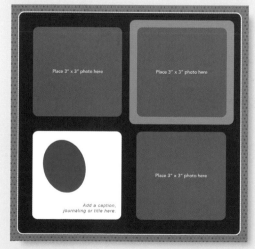

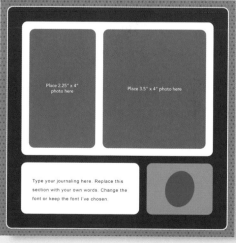

82schmfil1-edg.psd   8 x 8
82schmfil1.psd   8 x 8

82schmfil2-edg.psd   8 x 8
82schmfil2.psd   8 x 8

add a caption here

title.text

1" x 1"   1" x 1"   1" x 1"

Place 6.3" x 4.7" photo here

85schmttl-edg.psd   8.5 x 11
85schmttl.psd   8.5 x 11

Place 5.3" x 1.3" photo here

Place 2.4" x 2.5" photo here

Lorem ipsum dolor sit amet, consectetuer adipiscing elit. Nunc et risus. Suspendisse porta justo quis est. Proin rutrum justo id turpis. Aenean id nibh et lorem sollicitudin egestas. Fusce metus wisi, faucibus et, sagittis ac, viverra elementum, metus. Lorem ipsum dolor sit amet, consectetuer adipiscing elit.

1" x 1"

title.here

Place 5.3" x 2.1" photo here

Add a caption here

date

85schmded-edg.psd   8.5 x 11
85schmded.psd   8.5 x 11

1" x 1"

Place 7.9" x 5" photo here

.table entry 1
.table entry 2
.table entry 3
.table entry 4

85schmtoc-edg.psd   8.5 x 11
85schmtoc.psd   8.5 x 11

title.here

Place 5.3" x 7" photo here

Place 2.4" x 4.3" photo or journaling background here.

85schmsec-edg.psd   8.5 x 11
85schmsec.psd   8.5 x 11

Place 5.3" x 4.2" photo here

Type your journaling here. Replace this section with your own words. Change the font or keep the font we've chosen. Remember, these are your pages and your memories. Our schemes are blueprints designed to make digital scrapbooking quick and easy.

Place 5.3" x 4.2" photo here

85schmfil1-edg.psd   8.5 x 11
85schmfil1.psd   8.5 x 11

Place 5.3" x 3.5" photo here

Place 5.3" x 3.5" photo here

Type your journaling here. Replace this section with your own words. Change the font or keep the font we've chosen. Remember, these are your pages and your memories.

85schmfil2-edg.psd   8.5 x 11
85schmfil2.psd   8.5 x 11